Copyrights

Everything has been said before. Every idea finds its roots in other ideas. We all build on words that have been spoken or written by others, or on experiences we've shared with other people. Many of the words in this book, were inspired by observing nature, so again, not totally mine.

So, no old-fashioned copyrights on this book. If you want to use parts of this book, just be fair and acknowledge where you borrowed these words from. I believe in abundance and that we will only multiply if we share. So feel free to use parts of this book. And you're invited to give a fair share if you make some good money by borrowing from this book. To inspire you to be a creative writer yourself, the maximum you can borrow without written permission is 10% of this book. Want more? Get in touch and just ask!

Since a lot of this book was given to me whilst spending time in nature, it feels fair to give back to nature. A dream I have is to create a 'Forêt d'Amour' nearby my home village. Trees planted in the shape of a heart. A forest where people feel loved by nature or human beings. Or watch it from above and get inspired.

I will donate 10% of the net income of each book to 'Forêt d'Amour', aiming to have the funds to buy the land and plant the trees within 5 years.

Acknowledgements:

Daphne, my wife; for your ongoing love, friendship, support and believing in me.

Wessel, my son; for inspiring me and filling me with pride by the battles you've conquered.

My friends, teachers, my coaches, nature, even my enemies; for inspiring me with the ongoing lessons you so generously give.

Alex C. Verlek van Tienhoven, 2019, Châtillon-en-Diois, France

Credits & Info

Design – Ton Swart
Picture on front cover – Alex Verlek van Tienhoven
Picture on back cover – Marianne Louge
Contact info:
Alex Verlek van Tienhoven
www.coaching-works.nl
info@coaching-works.nl
First print May 2019

Published by Coaching Works International

Reading Suggestions

Of course it is totally up to you how to read this book, and if you're open to it, here are some suggestions how you could read and, most of all, use this book.

As mentioned in chapter 2, Awareness Builder, this book is hopefully going to make you reflect on the topics such as addressed in this book. With the intention to inspire you to make some positive changes through powerful choices.

After reading a chapter, give yourself some time to reflect on it. For this purpose each chapter is followed by a page with some questions with the invitation to chew on them and capture your own thoughts and insights. Use this page for journaling. Give it some time, there is no rush. And since very little is written in stone, it's OK to change your mind.

The combination of reading and journaling will deepen your awareness which hopefully leads to even more powerful and conscious choices around this topic. Your choices.

A choice without action is just a thought and will not bring the change you're longing for.
So the next step is to act. What will you start doing? Stop doing? What will you start saying, or maybe stop saying?
And sometimes the action is a change in your thought pattern, the way you look at something or someone.
My longing for you is that your thoughts and actions will transform into an even more authentic expression of yourself. No more playing small, half-truths or even total BS. When even addicts (see chapter 3) have an ultimate choice how to respond to the disease called addiction, and stop

being a victim of it, you too have the power to change and take charge over your own life.

Be kind to yourself when you try and fail. Just try again, taking in the lessons of your First Attempt In Learning. Powerful choices, kindness to self and perseverance are the path to sustainable change.

There is an 80% higher chance that you will follow up on the actions you chose to take, when you create some kind of accountability around it. Find someone with whom you share the choices you've made and the actions you've decided to take. And agree on a moment, or moments, where you will share how things are going. Find somebody who's not pampering you yet will be, maybe even painfully, curious about how things are developing. Find yourself a courageous accountability buddy!

So here again some reading suggestions:
Read – Reflect – Become Aware – Choose – Act – Be Accountable.
And make it an ongoing process. Because there are lessons to be harvested from the actions. Reflect on them. Deepen your awareness, make new choices and again, act accordingly.
And oh, don't forget to have fun during the process. Being grumpy and taking things, including yourself, too serious, will give you wrinkles and grey hair.

Index Awareness Builder 101

1 Discipline

The book you're reading now, didn't write itself.
At some point in time, I got the idea to write 52 short reflections of 500 words each. I'm not the kind of guy that can sit very long, not to read, nor to write. Yet I love it to capture my thoughts, feelings and experiences into words, so this felt like a nice compromise. So here you go, 52 times 500 words, the book is born.

I would build a statue for the person who invents an app that could capture all my ideas and thoughts in words. I've got like a billion ideas every day and I can make up a whole story just from one thing I see, one word, one insight. Life would be so much easier with such an app! But hey, here I find myself capturing the thoughts that I'm having right now on my cell phone. Just to avoid losing them.
I am on a hike with my dog Bibi through the vineyards and forests surrounding our house. Whilst enjoying the wind and the sun on my skin, the smells of fresh green after a mild shower in the night. The sounds of the birds, of my footsteps. I realise I even enjoyed the sound of my wife snoring during the night (the poor thing has a huge cold!).

Then I caught myself! It's happening again! *"You're in one of these funny moods where you get inspired by kind of everything. Yet by the time you get home, other things grab your attention and they get priority over sitting behind your desk and write down these words. Yes mister, if you want to make this book happen, to promote it from just one of your ideas to something tangible, you need to discipline yourself and start writing."*
Déjà vu!!! Discipline; during one of my previous funny reflective moods, I've been chewing on that word. What does it actually mean? And why is this one of the few words with three times the letter "I" in it?
And it was only when I started to write the word differently that my eyes

8

opened.....dIscIplIne.

That letter "I" points at me. Discipline is something you cannot delegate. It is 100% up to you! I mean, ME.

So often the best ideas are wasted and goals not met due to a lack of discipline. What a waste of opportunity.

It took me a long time to finally understand that punishment, not even self-punishment, won't stimulate us to reach our goals. Motivation can't come from a negative or external source. It needs to come from within, from within ourselves. True motivation will be born when we connect what's really important to us with the footprint we want to create in life. With our core and purpose. That's where 'have to' changes into 'want to'. That's when we're starting to make promises to ourselves and find the energy to keep going. When we promote that promise into a commitment to self, it is as if we sign this with a signature of our heart. Every heartbeat will bring us closer to our goal.

Discipline, written as dIscIplIne, is sticking to the commitment to self.

Journaling "Discipline"

What does commitment to myself mean for me?

Where do I try to delegate my discipline?

What choices do I want to make around discipline?

2 Awareness Builder

So, the book has been born. It's there. The question is why another book? What's the purpose of this book, of transforming some thoughts into words.

To me this book is a way, just one of them, to express the purpose I see for myself in life.

Some coaches, yes, I'm one of them, like to talk about life purpose. Many spiritual teachers also talk about the reason for our existence. So it's probably worthwhile to give it some thought...

When exploring this with my clients, I talk about footprint, impact and legacy. Here is some good news, you don't need to die to leave a legacy! So let's be light hearted about it and take a closer look.

Impact; there is no such thing as having no impact. Even before we were born we had impact. During our lives, everything we do, or not do, speaking or silent, when we are present or absent, it all has an impact. If we promote this to a fact, we'd rather be conscious about the impact we have.

Footprint. In a way in line with impact. Yet it's different. Where impact is more about how we are, footprint is the mark we leave behind.

Experienced trail hunters can not only tell by the footprint they find what kind of animal passed by, they can also tell a lot about when it was and how the animal was. Was it relaxed, in a hurry or even wounded. They can read a complete story in the footprint they see. Well, our footprints tell our story. And it is up to us what the story is that we write....

Legacy is what you leave behind for others to start creating from. Your output is their input.

My longing for you is that at the end of the journey, you've written not only the complete story, but also the story you really like it to be.

A story that you love to read to younger generations. A story that would fill your heart with joy when you read it.

With this book I want to leave you with more questions than answers. My longing is that my reflections get you wondering what that specific theme means to you. That you start looking for your answers. That you become more aware.
Awareness comes with a certain responsibility though. It forces you to choose. Will you choose to act in line with how you want your story to be, or not?
It's simple, act in line with it and you'll be very pleased with the book of life you're writing. And the opposite is also true I'm afraid.
This is where I find my purpose, the footprint I want to leave behind. I see myself as an 'awareness builder who creates an army of positive change'. I hope this book inspires you to make some positive changes through powerful choices.

So here again some reading suggestions:
Read – Reflect – Become Aware – Choose – Act – Be Accountable.
(Please don't forget to read the pages 4 and 5 where you'll find some additional thoughts around these suggestions)

Choose consciously so you make your life happen instead of life is just happening to you.

Journaling "Awareness Builder"

Where in my life am I longing for some change?

What is the obstacle between my choices and my actions?

How can holding myself accountable serve me ?

3 Weakness or Courage?

As the father of a recovering addict, I had the privilege to witness some NA-meetings. NA stands for Narcotic Anonymous, a gathering of people who're seeking each other's support whilst fighting a disease called addiction. Addiction, often perceived as a sign of weakness.

Each time I join such a meeting, I'm in awe. In awe with the courage. In awe with the simplicity. In awe with the power. In awe with the community. In awe with the fellowship.

Imagine, there is a part in your life that you're not happy with. Yes, pause for a moment and think about where you're doing something too much or too little. You're painfully aware it's not serving you yet it seems to control you. The worst thing you can imagine happening is this being taken away from you and that the world around you would know about your secrets. Would know about what you have done to fulfil this longing. Something that is so private, you don't even dare to be honest about it to your loved ones. Not to anyone, not even yourself. You live a lie. A lie leading to destruction. And, often for years, you've been denying this lie and you became a master in covering it up.

And here you are. In a group of people and all they want to hear is the naked truth. However ugly it is, that's just as it is. Your story will land in a bed of understanding, respect and love. In a space where the distinction is made between 'sin and sinner'. We hate the addiction, we love the addict. Because the addict is simply a human being, like you and me, longing for love and acceptance. Judgment is the last thing we're looking for.

And one of the ways these vulnerable yet so powerful men and women are supporting each other is by witnessing each other's stories. There is a unique kind of trust, allowing all to share whatever is on their heart. Whether it is a success or a struggle.

Successes are being celebrated, struggles are being acknowledged. Not the struggle itself, no, the human being who's courageous enough to simply share his or her struggle.

In one hour you hear many people sharing their stories. Each time starting with sharing their first name, let's say John, followed by "I'm an addict". That's being embraced by a collective 'hi John'. John is being seen, John is being heard. John gets a safe and courageous space to share what's on his heart. And 'all' they do is witness John's story. Nobody is trying to fix John nor comfort him. John is allowed to be, in his glory or in his struggle. Because John matters. Because no-one puts himself or herself above John. Because they're fellows.

In many cases addicts go on a daily basis to these meetings. To share. To be in this safe and courageous space. Let's assume you're not an addict in any shape or form. But since you're human, you have your shortcomings. And as spiritual teachers preach, a shortcoming is like any other shortcoming and that makes us all equal. How would it be to daily openly confess your shortcomings and struggles and put all your cards on the table. To embrace your imperfection and no longer keep up appearances?

Is that weakness or is that courage?

(For those who seek support, visit www.aa.org or www.na.org)

Journaling "Weakness or Courage?"

What is a behavioural pattern where I must make a courageous choice to break the spell?

What is the price I am paying by not doing so?

What will become possible if I choose to break the spell?

4 Time

The moment you were reading the title is just a few seconds ago, yet already gone. And that moment will never be back. Nor will be this moment. The clock might stop but the time always moves on.

Though there seems to be an endless amount of time, after every second that is now history, there will be a new one, right? On the scale of eternity, correct. On the scale of our life, hmm, there are many seconds but they are measured. Nor do we know how many seconds we'll get. In that sense, time is maybe the most precious thing we've been given. Yes, we get if for free, we receive it as a gift when we're born. Rich or poor, we all receive that gift. Time does not discriminate yet often we don't find it fair, after all, some of us have been given only very little time. Some of us have lost children and are painfully aware of the unfairness of time. I lost my father when he was only 53 and he still had lots and lots of plans for his life. And, he didn't get the seconds to live these plans....

When I'm writing these words, I am 53. The same age as when my father died. For sure it got me thinking when I turned 53. Some fear based questions like, will I outlive my father or will this also be my year...? Other questions helped me more. When observing my father's life, what lessons are there for me? Which choices did he make that he probably would have made differently if he would have known the number of his years. One of the lessons I took is about money. It feels my father's motto was to save his money wisely. I agree and I want to add 'spend it wisely'. A certain amount of money in the bank account is wise, not spending it to enjoy life a missed opportunity.

Another lesson is to enjoy life NOW! Yes, now! This is the only moment in time you are living. You can enjoy memories from the past, you can't go back in time to create an experience though. You can look forward to things, you can't fully experience what's still about to happen as if you are actually experiencing it now. Don't postpone harvesting the fruits life has to offer now, to another time. The fruit might be gone or that time might not come. Enjoy the gift of the present.

Another thing I became aware of is how I want to use my time, for instance whilst working. With time being one of the most precious gifts of life, let's use it well. Use it purposeful, use it to create the footprint you want to leave behind. When not, maybe that's the definition of wasting time?

Time, a limited resource.
Again, the clock might stop, time never will.

Journaling "Time"

How conscious and purposeful do I use my time?

What do I not want to regret at the end of my time?

What is the footprint I want to create whilst traveling through life?

5 Fragile

The evening I wrote the previous page, the friend of one of my students died. Far too young. Life was taken away from her, her time was complete. What a painful reminder.

A bit over a year ago I collapsed just like that and was taken to hospital by ambulance. Whilst enjoying breakfast at the local market, all of a sudden it felt as if all the energy fled from my body. My blood pressure all of a sudden was extremely high. When I was carried into the ambulance, I consciously looked at the sun and consciously felt its warmth on my skin. Maybe that was the last time I would see the sun from this side of heaven....
Yet I was lucky, it all proved to be a false alarm.

The night after writing the previous page, I woke up in the middle of the night. I felt horrible and again, all energy fled from my body. I went to sleep feeling great and happy, and only hours later, an extreme fear filled me. What is my body doing to me.....? Will it give up on me...? Is my time now complete...?
Again, false alarm. Again, a wake-up call. Yes, probably the rather intense last weeks impacted me, maybe even the writing yesterday caused some unconscious stress.

That's not the point. Stings' words in his song 'Fragile' are so spot on! We might think we're untouchable. We might be blessed with a good health, a strong body and a strong mind. And we are so fragile.... Nobody is too strong, too healthy or too important to not be told that, all of a sudden, your time is complete. That you will become one of the stars and life in this form will no longer know a new tomorrow.

Because on and on the rain will fall. Like tears from a star, the rain will say how fragile we are.
(from Fragile by Sting)

When a tear from a star falls on you, you're called to join the stars and we'll never know when we catch that tear. This calls for a certain humbleness. I am, you are, we are not better than anyone else and none of us is untouchable. We're all equally fragile.

When taking this as a given, when we are aware of our vulnerability, it doesn't call for living so careful that we avoid any risk. NO! We need to live!! When Snoopy's friend Charlie Brown said to him "One day we will die Snoopy....", in response Snoopy said: *"Yes, but every other day we will live..."*.

This is a simple wisdom, yet very powerful and it calls us forth to live our life. Fully. Now. Free. On purpose. Actively. Yet aware of how fragile we are and that one day we'll be called home to the stars. Embracing how fragile we are, at the same time encouraged to appreciate life more fully. Live it.

Journaling "Fragile"

What does a fully lived life look for me?

What am I allowing to get in the way of that?

If I would not be given a 'tomorrow', what would I do today?

6 The Unedited Version

Thank you for reading this far! It could be that you got inspired by what you've been reading and you're hoping for more thought provoking stuff. Simply keep reading with this mindset, I'm sure you will indeed find more of that.

It could be quite the opposite, where you find yourself less inspired or even bored. Simply keep reading with that mindset and I'm sure, I guarantee you, you'll find more of that stuff!

When you're in the mood for a little experiment, you could try reading with the opposite mind-set. Fair chance that you will start seeing things from the other perspective. Since, at the end of the day, perspective is a powerful choice, don't be surprised when you actually start experiencing different emotions around what you read, even exactly in the way you chose to look at it.

Some spiritual teachers describe the fact we're able to choose how we see and experience whatever happens in life, as the gift of ultimate freedom. Of course, this I don't want to take away from you...

I believe that in essence I am not even able to do so, nor could anyone else. You might be influenced by someone else, at the end of the day it still is your choice.

This is actually the whole point of this book; to make you aware of certain topics, that you start reflecting on it and that you consciously choose how to see things. Whatever I write, how I write it, it doesn't really matter that much. My main longing for you is that you find your own inspiring way to see things. So when you're not inspired by what you read, start exploring how you would like to be inspired around that topic. If you're not inspired by how things are being worded, please challenge your thoughts how you would have worded it.

Also when you are inspired by what you read, explore more deeply what's been evoked in you that makes you feel inspired. That way you'll deepen your learning and make it more consciously yours. Do not simply accept or even embrace it at first sight! No! Take what you read and after reflecting on it, make these words your own authentic words, thoughts and feelings.

That's why this book has the subtitle 'The Unedited Version'. These are my authentic words, my current perspective. It was a conscious choice to not ask an editor to 'polish' my words. It would simply take away from the authenticity of it. A gift of having this book edited, would be that it would evoke more thinking in me and new insights. Then I could rewrite my words to update them. Before publishing, the editor would look at it again and since the editor, in the meantime also processed the words and own thoughts and feelings around it, would also have new insights again. See what could happen? We would be able to keep rewriting and editing, create a never ending loop and never get to the point of publishing.

This would be the ultimate victory for my saboteurs - my inner critics who don't want me to step into new things - who'd love to say it could always be better. In itself that's correct. Their victory would be that you would never be reading this book, that your thoughts would never be evoked by it. Hence, no change, the ultimate goal of saboteurs.

So here you are, reading the unedited version, a victory over my saboteurs!

And now, please create your own unedited authentic version of the words you're reading.

Journaling "The Unedited Version"

Where am I allowing others or circumstances to write the story of my life?

What does the unedited version of my life story look like?

For that matter, what do I want to embrace and what to let go of?

7 Perfectionizm

The saboteurs were not done yet! They felt they were losing the battle around this book being edited or not. They just hate losing! When they lose, change of some form is happening which will make them feel as if they're sleeping on an ant hill. No, that's not nice…!
So they had to think of something else and tried several options. Like "who do you think you are that anyone would be inspired by your words"? Sorry guys, after I got over myself when I started leading courses, that one doesn't land anymore.

Next attempt: "These thoughts are rather personal, do you really want the whole world to see all that"? Hi hi, the whole world you say? If my book would be that successful, I'd be rich in one go! Great! And besides that, I'm far too eccentric to be bothered by that.
Then they played their ultimate card: "Alex, English is not your mother tongue. You will make silly mistakes and printed words should be at least correctly written".
You freaking bastards! Playing the card of perfectionism totally sucks!!
I'm using such strong words because I know there is truth in what they say. Mistakes will be made! Not even the best spelling check software will be able to avoid that. Maybe eventually the spelling will be correct, but some things will not always be worded in the best possible way.
Hmm, maybe not an editor, but at least a corrector then?

It's very liberating to embrace not to be perfect. And at the same time I know that in my work I have rather high standards for myself. Of course it's OK to strive for a really good result, and I know I can overdo that.
It's the paralysing impact of perfectionism my saboteurs were after.
Perfectionism is a guaranteed path to self-imprisonment. It is the thief

of freedom. It's hijacking satisfaction. It's the sniper that kills ideas, the tsunami that ruins creativity.

As a facilitator of international courses, I so often tell my students it's not a language course, as long as we come from a mutual desire to communicate, we'll be fine! When we do our best, it'll be good enough. And our best, that's all we can do.

When we aim for more than our best, we make life impossible. No, that's not an invitation to go for second best. Then we underperform and won't respect our talents.

In the battle against perfectionism, I hold on to a quote on a poster we have in our house; "Strive for excellence, not for perfectionism". Of course, give it your best shot, aim high! Embrace your full potential and at the same time relax into it. Don't torture yourself expecting the impossible which means you're constantly disqualifying yourself. Always saying "what I did wasn't perfect, not good enough" will soon evolve into "I'm not good enough". And that is an absolute lie!

After giving it all you've got, embrace the result as your best and release it into the world. Declare it ready.

After giving it your utmost and declaring it 'good enough' implies declaring yourself good enough.

And with that you free yourself from perfectionizm.

Journaling "Perfectionizm"

How am I allowing my perfectonizm to steal away my freedom?

What is the illusion I'm making up how this is serving me?

What choices must I make to break free from my Saboteurs?

PS: Play with the Sabogram in the Appendix to disempower your Saboteurs

8 The Myth of the Comfort Zone

We all know it, right? That place where it feels light and safe, easy and calm. That special space where we can just hang out. Just chill. Nothing is happening there. It's that place where we don't feel challenged. Not by change, not by questions, not by others. Not even by ourselves.

It's that funny, little place where we can just be. It's so nice and comfi that we could easily fall asleep here.

And actually, that's exactly what's happening there! We think we are awake, alive even, yet in reality we're asleep. Even with our eyes wide open. We're asleep and we're being fooled. We're even in serious danger. Because this comfort-zone has walls and they are moving. Slowly yet constantly. We don't notice it and if we notice anything, it's a false sense of safety. For a long time it felt this place was warming up, bit by bit and we appreciated the warmth. It seems to change from an open place with an unpleasant draft, to a place where the temperature slowly rises to a nice, comfortable kind of warmth.

In the meantime, in reality, with the walls of this place slowly closing in on us, the pressure builds up. It's like a steam-cooker. More and more air but in less and less space. Yet, there is no pressure valve. Initially we notice that the draft disappears and that the temperature slowly goes up. We're clueless why, but hey, it's comfy so why bother? It must be right!

And then there is that day where we feel like stretching, maybe even jump around a bit, to then discover that your moving space is limited. Weird, we don't get why. It's probably just one of these off days. We simply skip moving or even lay down again. See, that weird feeling fades away. All is good again.

In the meantime the walls, even the ceiling and the floor keep creeping towards the middle. Invisible yet not unnoticed. Slowly we notice our breathing gets heavier. Strange. Let's go and see a doctor. Ask for some pills. This tension that's building up can't be healthy. Probably too much stress, Pills, maybe alcohol or even drugs will release the tension. Or a good sick leave. We might have a burn-out.

In a way, that's right! You are burning out of life! Bit by bit you allow your energy streams to glide into a coma... Why?!? Because you're in the zone of self-limitation! That lethally dangerous zone where you're heading towards an implosion of self. Your system is screaming to break free from limiting beliefs, restrictions imposed upon self. The comfort zone is just one big fraud! Driven by self-sabotage and false beliefs.

And now you're at choice. Are you going to break down these walls of the zone of self-limitation or will you accept this slowly lethal prison. Are you going to listen to your heart, your body, your soul, all of them crying to break free? Are you going to step into freedom and an unlimited space to move and create? Or not?

Alive? Or dead whilst still breathing.

Your call.

Your life.

Journaling "The Myth of the Comfort Zone"

Where is my system screaming to break free from limiting beliefs, restrictions imposed upon myself?

What does an unlimited space where I can move and create freely look like?

What is actually the full range of my authentic self?

9 Holiday

No, I am not in a grumpy mood! And yes, I think holiday is a totally misunderstood concept!

The weeks before we leave, we work our ass off. We're convinced that after our holiday there will be 'the big nothing' or at least it'll be too late for almost everything and we for sure need to close that last deal. It's our last chance after all! We're stressed out and sleep really bad. We have these stupid arguments with the people we love and are supposed to go on a holiday with. We need to go and see our mother since it's not really acceptable, after months of forgetting about her, to leave without saying goodbye.

We race to the airport and hate all these other idiots who are also stressed out whilst going to the same airport. Or, when we've decided to drive it's even more interesting. We get up at 3 AM to avoid the horrible traffic jams to find out we're not the only ones who had that brilliant idea. So by the time we get to the French motorway, the kids are monsters and mom and dad are no longer talking to each other. The only reasonable voice in the car comes from the navigation system who tells us it's only another 666 kilometres to our destination. This is hell!

Back 'talking' we argue that we've been working hard all year and spending far too much money on this damned holiday. Yes, the perfect way to start these most special weeks of the year... Not!!

I'm thinking back of my grandfather. Born in 1900. Died at the blessed age of 82 when he stepped on his bike to go and buy milk. Instead he went to heaven. Reflecting on his life, how he created balance, I also started to wonder why he wasn't stressed out because he never went on a holiday.

Here are my observations. He understood the word holiday and its origin really well. Holiday comes from the words Holy Day. A day set aside to rest, to spend time with the family, to do NOTHING! Time to worship and reflect. Yes, he was a religious man so he also went to church, but those who were not religious followed a similar pattern. They set aside time for the other important things in life. Everything other than work.

In addition, they created some holiday in every day. Even though 12 hours working days were pretty normal, they had their little moments of rest in every single day. Blessed with not having TV nor smartphone, they had time to talk with each other whilst having diner, whilst drinking coffee in the evening. To read a book. To tell stories. To simply stare out of the window. To walk to the fence and observe the sheep. To pray or simply be silent.

A little holy time makes every day a holy day. Granting yourself that, when you then go for your holiday, you might be able to enjoy that even more.....

Journaling "Holiday"

How relaxed, or stressed do I start my holiday and what do I make up about that?

Where do I find a bit of holy day in every day?

How do I choose to start my next holiday?

10 Recovering Calvinist

Sometimes things don't go as planned. After some calls in the morning, I was supposed to see somebody in the afternoon. It had been a really long time since I saw this person and I was really looking forward to this reunion. Sometimes it just happens that you bump into someone where it feels like there is a click from the start. Then my 'gypsy lifestyle' continues, so I often never see that person again, or it takes years.

Providence brought us close to each other and we decided to benefit from the occasion and carve out time together. To reconnect, to catch up and to see what the future might hold. Next to catching up on a personal level, I was also curious what we could create together professionally. Whatever the outcome would be, I was looking forward to this moment! After finishing my calls I sent a message where to meet and decided to enjoy the sun whilst overlooking the Mediterranean. It was just a narrow street and the beach of Sitges between me and the sea. Then a message arrived from my friend; something with one of the kids came up, meeting cancelled. Just like that, all plans ruined.

Carved out a whole afternoon..... After all these years..... Several other thoughts crossed my mind. Disappointment and frustration took over. To the point I almost started feeling sorry for myself......

Man, wake up! Get your act together and don't let this ruin your afternoon, your day even! Look in front of you. Sea, beach, people, aliveness, some free time!

A few minutes later I found myself walking on the beach, wow, can't remember how long ago that was. Walking on the beach of Sitges, there could be worse 'punishments' for a cancelled appointment! On the beach I started looking for shells, like I did as a kid. I was surprised, I didn't find any. Just tiny, tiny shells. I looked up and also found many people without 'shells'. Both genders felt free to show bellies and breasts, no need to hide anything. Couples in all thinkable combinations kissing on the beach, because they are in love. Another doing yoga exercises on the end of a peer. A mother breastfeeding her baby. Bodies in all shapes and sizes were shown freely. A group of elderly ladies doing aqua aerobics. People were just doing what they felt like doing. Nobody felt they needed to hide anything, nobody needed a shell to hide in. Everybody could simply be themselves. Nobody took offence. Agreeing or not wasn't relevant, just be your wonderful self.

I found a nice place close by the sea to reflect and enjoy the sun and the wind on my skin.
Then I realised what I needed to learn this afternoon. I thought I already freed myself from a lot of the limiting protestant, Calvinistic beliefs I was brought up with. The shell I needed to get out was the shell of 'thou shalt' or 'thou shan't'. Thou should always keep your promises. Thou shouldn't kiss at certain places. And so on. I was shocked. Why did I even notice all the things listed above. Because they went through my old Calvinistic 'thou should (not)-filter'.
Recovered Calvinist. I thought so. This shell seems to be stubborn. But I will break free! Now! And as often as needed.
Guess I'm not the only 'shell-fish'. We create many shells; fear, judgement, shame, worry, not worthy, it's an endless list.
We are not born to be a shell-fish, we are born to be free!

Journaling "Recovering Calvinist"

What's the shell I want to free myself from?

How am I judging myself or others whilst in my shell?

Who can I become when living free from my shell?

11 The Magic of Silence

When I think about why the universe changed the course of my life when coaching found me, one of the answers that keeps coming back is that I needed to learn a lot about myself. I also needed a lot more preparation to deal with what life still had in store for me.

Though coaching found me in my early forties, and I considered myself as a grown up man, it became very clear that I needed a big list of additional skills.

I must admit, I always thought I was pretty smart with words. Not often I didn't know what to say and when I spoke, it was often smart and convincing. Even funny from time to time.

Now it feels that convincing was frequently actually overpowering, using smart words, sharp words, position or posture as tools to get it my way. I describe this as competitive communication where the aim is to win. Listening was actually analysing and measuring the others' words to find out how I could use them for my personal gain. Listening was done through the filters of gaining and losing, right or wrong, enemy or friend.

Often the words never got much further than my brain, the place where logic lives.

Whilst being trained as a Co-Active coach, I learned about multiple ways to listen. A real breakthrough happened when I somehow realised why we have two ears and only one mouth. Guess why that would be...???

Maybe a simple conclusion could be that it might be a good idea to listen twice as much as that we speak. And since it feels I have some catching up to do here, I'm aiming for a different ratio. Even more listening and even less talking.

One place I discovered to be a very good environment to practice listening, is in nature. As often as possible I go into nature, preferably on my own, which makes it even easier to not speak.... With listening being the only option left, I started to listen to the silence. The sounds of silence. The gifts of silence. Have you ever been sitting in a forest very early in the morning or when it's getting dark? That moment where the birds welcome the day or sing to say it goodbye and welcome the night. When you are so silent you can hear a roe deer approaching, a mouse between the leaves. Or even your own heartbeat.

This only becomes possible when you reach a state of silence, that you start listening with your soul. And a deep, intimate way of communication opens up when we start listening this way to other people. When we allow the words we hear, or even the silence we hear, to not only be filtered by our minds for meaning, but also by our whole body, our heart and our soul, as if we become like one big ear. That's when we start hearing, no actually experiencing much more of the message the other human being is transmitting. And it's then often our silence that forms the next question, not our words.

In silence we can learn to listen, not only to hear, not only to understand but to accept and connect.

Journaling "The Magic of Silence"

What is my heart longing for to hear?

What can I hear in the silence?

Where in my life do I want to practice more WAIT (Why Am I Talking)?

12 (I'm)Perfect

From time to time it shows up, that so called liberating reframe of the word imperfect. With a bit of 'creativity' the word 'imperfect' transforms into 'I'm Perfect'.

Come on, who are we fooling here?!

I've got some shocking news, NOBODY is perfect. Nobody, meaning not a single person in the world. Even those who look into the mirror and come to the conclusion that 'if perfect doesn't exist, it doesn't get much closer than the person I'm looking at now", you're simply underlining that nobody is perfect.

This whole 'I'm Perfect' nonsense to me simply proves we're unable to embrace our human nature. We just find it too hard to embrace our shortcomings. Making mistakes, breaking rules or even the law, lying, forgetting, even screwing up completely, it's all part of life!

I think being perfect would also be utterly boring! Never again wondering whether you will succeed or fail.... Always knowing in advance that whatever you do, whatever you try will work out without any shortcoming, not a single error at all. Every exam we take, we know beforehand we get the maximum score.

Without feeling the sadness of a failed exam or a failed attempt, we would never be able to experience the joy of succeeding. It would just be normal. Imagine that this exciting anticipation, this wondering will it work out or not, will be stolen away from you? This would also steel away the joy of succeeding, of passing that exam or whatever thing we tried out..... Remember that 'joy-gasm' the last time you heard that great news of succeeding? When you screamed from the top of your lungs a raw and loud 'YES'!! Your heart-beat went up and you were dancing with joy.

Well, being perfect will steal that away from you. It'll simply make you an emotional flat liner. Emotionally dead.

Another thing. Let's imagine for a moment you found the perfect partner. Your partner's words, acts, moves, looks, silence, clothes, everything would be just perfect. I would just freaking hate myself since I'll never be able to keep up, to feel equal to that annoyingly perfect partner!

OK, imagine that you too are a perfect partner. So never any arguments again, hmm, boring! And on top of that, it would steal away good old make-up sex, nah, that could never have been the idea behind a good and alive relationship.

There's a third scary thought. Next to a totally boring, joy-less, predictable, emotionally flat life without make-up sex, we would lose so many chances to learn. We need to be imperfect to make mistakes whilst mistakes are a door-opener to learn and grow. To learn and be creative whilst trying out new ways. I believe in the old wisdom that where we fall, often the biggest treasures can be found. Or that acronym, FAIL: First Attempt In Learning. We need to fail, we need to be imperfect in order to learn.

So here is a small test you can do to decide if you really want to be perfect.

I want a life without:
❏ Joy
❏ Make-up sex
❏ Learning

If you tick one or more of the boxes, I wish you good luck on your path to perfection.

If you tick none of the boxes, just get over yourself and embrace your human state of imperfection.

Journaling "(I'm)Perfect"

Where do I long to let go of my perfectionism?

How is my perfectionism an obstacle to freedom and joy?

How is my perfectionism an obstacle towards my relationships?

13 JOY IS

All my Facebook posts start with these two words. And then it describes something that brings a smile to my face. Accompanied with a picture of that moment, that view, that feeling.

The posts were born in response to the countless posts with political or religious opinionated messages. Agreeing or disagreeing with a certain politician. Trying to convince the world about how God sees something, to be more religious, in a different way, or why you shouldn't be religious. Another favourite topic; things that go wrong in the world where we of course need to share our opinion. In reaction to those opinions, on either of the above topics, more opinions. Pro, con, left, right.... It is as if I'm reading another newspaper or magazine. We've got enough of those!

Once I saw a cartoon which was also spot-on! A waiter in a restaurant asked the couple if there was something wrong with their food since they hadn't taken a picture to post on Facebook yet. Aaagh, as if I care you're eating Brussels sprouts, a steak, or spaghetti?!! Drinking a beer or a cocktail?!! Well, not the slightest bit....sorry.

What I do care about, is if you're finding joy in life. Joy, that feeling that makes your heart sing. That makes your eyes water. That brings a smile to your face. That makes you cuddle up with that person next to you. That makes you slow down for a moment. That makes you want to sing or dance. Or both!

And when you witness other people enJOYing life, for just that brief moment, it often also brings a bit of joy to your heart. Try it, open up for it.

In response to my series of JOY IS posts, people sometimes wonder if life is just one big party for me. Always joy? That can't be!?! And they are correct, as much as they are mistaken.

I do know my share of struggles. For instance, my body decided to have fibromyalgia, meaning that there is not a single day without pain. I lost a parent at a rather young age. I had a totally failed marriage with two kids, with all the troubles that come with that. I have three grandchildren and of two of them I don't even know their names. I've been ill for more than two years which still carries its scars. And I can go on. Like you could create your long list of struggles and challenges. We're the same. Life sometimes isn't funny at all. If that's where your focus is....

When the doctor told me about my fibromyalgia and that there is nothing I could do to make it better, I decided to prove her wrong. Instead of having the focus on my pain, I decided to focus on the gifts of life. The moments I'm touched by something beautiful, something fun, something special. It's usually found in something that's not costing any money, and very widely available. It's to be found in the 'simple' things of life.

JOY IS for free, all you need to do is put your focus on it. And it'll soften many, many pains and fears....

Journaling "JOY IS"

What is an area in my life where I could do with more JOY?

What is JOY for me?

I choose to add more JOY to my day by....?

14 My Owner

Questions. In general we aim to answer them instantly. The faster the better. That's also the expectation with which we ask questions. We want instant answers, solutions, clarity. Nothing wrong with it!! In most cases that's exactly what I want myself. I have a question and I need an answer so I can move forward.

Yet sometimes, a question really deserves it to marinate in time. These aren't the questions which are asked to give an answer to the person who asked. No, they are a gift for the one receiving the question. It's meant to send the receiving person on a rich journey of exploration. Hours, days or even weeks of chewing on that question. Whilst there is no right or wrong answer, yet with time the answer usually evolves. Layer after layer opens up with time. It's a bit philosophical, maybe even a spiritual journey of self-exploration. Finding an answer and questioning it right away. Because something inside you tells you there is more to be discovered. It's like a good wine where time is an essential part of its richness.

Recently I was given such a question: "Who is your owner". Just 4 simple words. And I 'wrestled' with those words for weeks. Who. Is. My. Owner.? Eventually two answers remained: I and God. Or was it God and I? Hmm, a new question came from the answer. I decided after a few days that the order didn't matter. I came to that conclusion after asking a 3rd and a 4th question: "What does it actually mean if I am my owner?" And: "Or when God is my owner?".

Being someone's possession initially felt limiting, not free. Yet I see God as the Divine Power, Spirit and Love who trusts me and loves me unconditionally. So much that I've been given the free choice what to make of my life. Isn't that the ultimate gift towards freedom, towards life? Feeling that Power, Spirit and Love makes that it doesn't matter anymore whether it's God or I who owns me. We're in this together!

Then owner God asked: "Do you love him as much as I do? Do you dare

to love yourself with Divine Spirit, Power and Love?"
These questions moved me deeply. Yet the answer was "no, not fully",
I didn't feel judged by it. On the contrary, it was an invitation, an
encouragement! If you want to please your owners, dare to love yourself.
Dare to grow and bear fruit. Dare to explore what life has in store for you.
Explore and live. Oh yes, that includes making mistakes. They are meant
to teach you important lessons so embrace your mistakes as an essential
part of your journey. It's part of the plan.
Moved by all this, one question remained towards my owners: "How to
live up to their expectations?"

God took the lead in answering: "Just do your best". I agreed.
Me cried with relief.

Journaling "My Owner"

What's the deal I want to close with my owner(s)?

Do I dare to love myself with Divine Spirit, Power and Love? If so, how? If not, what's getting in the way?

What choices do I want to make in order to judge myself less and simply embrace all I can do is my best?

15 Respect

More than 10 kilometres up in the air. In a huge bird. Unless you're a smart ass engineer you just can't figure out how this impressive Boeing 777-200 is ever able to lift off. Hundreds of people get on board. I'm just one of them. After working for a few days in Seoul, South Korea, I'm heading back home. A long journey with two flights and several hours of driving home before I'll finally, way after midnight, be able to wrap myself around my loved one. Feeling her skin against mine, her warm body against mine. Safely home, in the comfort of my own house surrounded by love. Whether it be a partner, pets, the furniture, home and comfort is what we long for, pretty sure that's one thing all passengers have in common.

We're flying through time zones, crossing huge countries like China and Russia before we'll be landing in Paris after more than 11 hours of flying.
Another thing all people on board during this long flight share, is a desire for comfort, for being treated like an appreciated guest. On this flight I'm one of the lucky ones. After a long time of collecting miles and adding an acceptable amount, I could upgrade to business class. An unknown luxury to me and I'm enjoying myself like a little child.

Until.... I see how some of the fellow 'lucky ones' are responding to the crew. The flight attendants who are doing their very, very best to treat us like royals. OK, I know it's their job but come on, they are human beings like you and me. They too are looking forward to the moment they're opening their front door and wrap themselves around a loved one.

I've travelled the world, explored many different countries and cultures. And one of the things all the people I've met have in common, is the desire to be respected. Whether it's the beggar in the street, hotel staff, the waiter or waitress, the taxi driver or the flight attendant, they all have a deeply rooted desire to be respected.

Who the fuck (yes, happy to not have an editor!) do we think we are to treat the people who're serving us like shit! Why do we treat them less, or even slightly different than for instance the boys and girls wearing fancy clothes whilst in their CEO-roles? Why do we think we can ask things above and beyond reason from flight attendants, from anyone serving us? Just because we're paying? Sorry, it just pisses me off!

Respect is born in seeing every human being as equal. No matter role or position. We're all born naked, we'll all die alone. To make the journey in between these moments more pleasant, let's remember we are all just human beings with a desire to be respected.

My definition of respect is 'treat everyone as you want to be treated'. If you want to be treated like royals, treat those who serve you like royals. If you want to be treated like shit.....you got the picture.

Journaling "Respect"

What's my definition of respect?

Where do I allow or tolerate disrespect?

Where do I catch myself treating others not that respectful?

16 Magic

When I want some 'no brain-time' I like to watch some 'whatever country got talent' on YouTube. Part of the fun is the jury. Some weird behaving guys like Simon 'what's his name' or the hot ladies next to him. I admit. The advantage of watching it on YouTube is that I can simply choose the parts that amuse me. Like a father and a son singing that harmonious, self-composed song moving me to tears. Or that guy with his funny cloths and 'wrong' glasses who happens to have adopted 6 kids with special needs and performing the most beautiful song so the jury can't help themselves but having to hit that golden buzzer. The only time I'm watching these shows is when I'm alone in my hotel room after leading a course. Just for fun. People doing something they are passionate about, they believe in. What then becomes possible is a kind of magic!

And, you don't have to be on that show to create magic!! When I'm leading courses and train people coaching-skills, we talk about things that are close to our heart. What is it that brings a smile to your face? What is it that excites you? What moves your heart? What makes you feel fulfilled? Wait a minute; what do these questions mean to you? STOP READING! NOW! Put this book aside and start chewing on these questions. No kidding, stop reading now and reflect on these three short questions. As long as you need.

OK, I hope you found a few answers, so let's continue.
When we connect from our core to what moves us, what brings a smile to our face, to what's close to our heart, we're going to experience magic. Your magic. You don't need to be a magician, a gifted singer, a dancer or talented in any of the fine arts to be magical.
Magic lives inside all of us, yes, that includes YOU! With total admiration for people with the talent to perform on stage, I'm also in awe with your

magic. When you connect with whom you are at your core and start creating magic from there. Every single one of us has something special to bring to this world. It's maybe not your talent as a singer or your skills as an acrobat, or anything like that. Very likely magic is happening because of what you're doing every single day. Like my friend who's an osteopath and with some 'simple' moves making people feel much better. Or my friend who's a teacher whose patience make kids blossom. Or my friend who's driving handicapped kids to school, so they have a great day. Or my wife, with her eye for detail making people feel welcome and seen.

Or you, with that one thing you do because it matters to your heart, to make a difference to that one person you meet. Magic isn't a show. Life is magic. When you live what moves your heart.

Journaling "Magic"

How am I bringing magic to the world?

What's a talent I have, that I want to express more?

Which choices do I want to make to no longer play small and create magic?

17 I'm sorry

Very important words to say. After we've done something that is disappointing someone. Letting someone down. When we're in somebody's way. Or even hurt somebody. There are many occasions where it's essential to take responsibility for our intended or unintended impact and simply say "I'm sorry". Well, simply... who was it, who wrote a song about sorry being the hardest word....?

Often, it's our ego that gets in the way of saying sorry. Our pride, our image is more important than admitting we screwed up. And with that usually making the situation bigger than needed. Very often people get more upset by us not admitting we messed up and apologising for it than the actual mistake. OK, probably that's not news to you. And if it is, you just found a bonus....

Then I got to know mr. D.

He is a purser on one of the world's major airlines. This wonderful man broke a record! He said "I'm sorry" or in French "Je suis désolé' more often in a few minutes than I ever heard before! Did he make so many mistakes? Were so many things going wrong? Was Murphy's law happening?

None of the above! It was nothing but his humble kindness that made him apologise. And in a way I respect him for it. Like many people say "I'm sorry" just because something is not going in the way somebody else is expecting. It takes a lot of self-management and/or professionalism to say "I'm sorry" even when you didn't do anything wrong. Like a friend of mine, who also listens to the name 'sunshine', and is a 'maître de cabine' for another wonderful airline and sometimes shares tiny bits about how often "I'm sorry' is needed to make somebody else feel better.

AND: How would the world change if we would only expect 'sorry' when someone actually made a mistake? And in all other situations either look for our own part in the thing going 'wrong' or when it's just bad luck or simply what it is, not complain and embrace it as part of life. Since life isn't freaking perfect and sometimes things are just different from what we may have expected.

Let's just ask ourselves what it requires from us to look at life this way.

AND: How would the world change if we would indeed take responsibility for all these moments where we do screw up and authentically say "I AM SORRY". Just admit we did something, or did not do something, said or not say something that was needed at that moment. Embrace our human imperfection. Nobody is perfect so everybody needs to say "I'm sorry" from time to time.

And, let's keep these special words for those moments where it's really necessary. Where we do need to take responsibility for our shortcomings.

Journaling "I'm sorry"

What does "I am sorry" mean to me?

When am I saying "I'm sorry" where I didn't make a mistake?

When am I not saying "I'm sorry" where I actually did make a mistake?

18 The lesson of the garden

Before starting my working day, I like to do some little things in our vegetable garden. Just some quiet time, only surrounded by the sounds of nature. The day slowly waking up. No emails yet. The plants, birds, sometimes some thoughts about the new day, often not even. It's like meditation. The 'nothingness' before 8 or more hours of work waiting for me. Precious moments.

Whilst spending time in the vegetable garden, it may seem not much is happening. The plant will not look much different from yesterday nor will the fruits or vegetables grow overnight. Not even the weeds seem to be in a hurry.

Yet, I'm mistaken. Nature is constantly in action. There is always something changing and when I take a closer look, I start to see things better. Or for the first time. These wonderful moments when you discover that plant starts to blossom, preparing to give food. Rewards for the time and work put into the garden.

The garden holds huge lessons in patience and trust. And commitment because the garden will only give you something when you dedicate time and effort to it. It's the gardener who needs to prepare the soil and creates the best possible environment for the plants to grow. Often that's hard labour, boring and repetitive.

You need to start well in advance. In some cases you need to think about the next season even before this season is over. You need to collect the seeds of the plants who just gave you fruit or vegetables. Collect, dry and store them. Label what it is and study how you need to treat them and find out what's the right moment to sow them again.

You need to fertilise the soil, spade it and then let it rest. Trim where needed. Clean and repair your tools. Build a greenhouse.

When the time is ready, sow the seeds, plant new plants. Protect the new green against invaders or unexpected cold. Give it water when needed, not too much, not too little.

When things start growing, you need to choose which plant you will give priority over the other. You totally understand that when you think you can get it all, you will get much less or even nothing. One will steal away energy from the other or totally choke it.

Then, harvest time! When you're ready at the right moment, you will be richly rewarded. Sometimes all comes at the same time and you need to work long hours. Sometimes you even have so much of one kind, you need to give it away to others because you don't want it to go to waste. And sometimes things don't go well for you, but since you've always shared from your abundance, this time your neighbour is happy to share with you.

Entrepreneurs and co-workers; you are like the gardener. Your market, your department is like your garden. Your colleague isn't your competitor but your neighbour.

Journaling "The lesson of the garden"

What does it take to treat my colleague / competitor / husband / wife / kids as my neighbour?

How do I share with others to increase collective wellbeing?

How much do I live by the lessons of the garden?

19 Bad bosses

Frequently I hear stories about how bad somebody's boss is. He, or she, upsets people by what he does, doesn't do, says, doesn't say. By being there or by being absent at unexpected moments. By allowing something today but tell you the opposite the next day. By a lack of compliments yet generous with complaints. By having favourites and by having some colleagues which he can't stand; and clearly showing that.

By blaming others for his own mistakes. By being deaf for suggestions. By taking the best holiday weeks as well as keeping the Christmas gifts received from other companies all to himself. And probably you have other examples when you think back of that annoying boss you once had. Or currently have..... Poor you!

Or, do you simply get the boss you deserve? If he gets the space to be such a horrible boss, what does that say about you? What is it in you, that you tolerate this kind of annoying behaviour?

Before you respond with the famous 'Yes, but...' and then give multiple reasons why it is the way it is, that there's nothing you can do about it, let's pause for a second.

There seems to be something toxic in this relationship. Yes, relationship. You are in a relationship with your boss. Of course, there is a hierarchy, yet you said 'Yes' to this job and by staying or not taking a stand, you accept it. Ok, maybe you can't leave today (well, just check with yourself how true that actually is....), yet what are you doing to create an 'escape plan'? When was the last time you gave him feedback and told him about the impact his behaviour has on you?

Or are you staying because you consciously want to learn from this situation so you can be a better boss by the time it's your turn.

Are you keeping a diary with 'lessons learned'?

Are you reflecting on your boss's behaviour so you can design a profile of the leader you want to be?

In case none of the above is applicable, you're not an employee, you're a slave. Which is illegal since a 'few' years.... And it is not the boss who is doing that, you allow it yourself. It is you, or me, who do not take a stand. It is not our boss who's ultimately responsible, we are responsible ourselves.

With accepting this unacceptable behaviour, you are your own worst boss and enslave yourself.

Yes, I know, there are some, let's be polite, not so nice people out there who are trying to lead a team and, since they have been promoted to their maximum level of incompetence, they fail. And being in such a team, having such a boss, simply sucks.

You don't deserve a boss, you deserve a leader. One who cares about you and for you. Who puts their people first.

And in order to get such a leader, you may have to be a leader of yourself first.

Journaling "Bad bosses"

What does leadership mean to me?

Where and how do I need to take the lead?

Where is it time I start to say "yes" or "no" in order to get the leader I deserve?

20 Smartphone

Sunday. In the summer time that means work, at least to my wife. The fun thing about lunchbreaks where we live, is that they are frequently up to two hours long. What do you mean, a quick bite from a sandwich ham/ cheese from the drawer in your desk? No, for lunch the French take their time and if possible, in a restaurant.

We do our utmost to integrate in the culture, so I suggested I would come to pick her up and go out for lunch together. Yes, sometimes adapting to another culture is 'hard work'.....

We had a simple, but good lunch whilst enjoying sitting on the terrace and the nice and relaxed atmosphere. At some point a family joined, young parents with two gorgeous small girls and a baby boy. I can't help myself but totally enjoying such a picture perfect, again also impressed how well French children behave in restaurants.

Whilst daddy was helping the girls ordering, the mother prepared a bottle for baby-boy. All so cute and what a joy to witness!

A couple of minutes later the hungry baby-boy had finished his lunch and was resting in his mother's arms. The rest of the family was waiting for theirs. The girls were doing their own thing and the baby just looked around a bit. Mom and Dad were fully focussed. Not on each other or their lovely kids, no, on their damned smartphones! Or should we say, on their freaking 'stupid-phones'....?

Whilst being absorbed by whatever it was on their phone, there was no contact whatsoever with the children, nor with each other. All that seemed to matter was their phone and because of that, totally missing the gift of the breathtakingly beautiful picture of their gorgeous kids. Missing that short yet very special moment babies are at their cutest.

What do you mean 'social' media.......

Over and over we witness these kind of moments. A couple in a restaurant, hardly speaking with each other yet fully available for the rest of the world. Deaf and blind for their partner, yet very curious to anything Facebook, Instagram or WhatsApp has to say. Or that email which, for sure, cannot be responded to the next day....

Or the phone became the way to keep kids occupied and, with their pale, blueish faces they are totally occupied by that funny movie on YouTube, preferably with the volume so high that everybody around them can listen in, whether they are interested or not.

Did you also noticed the first question we ask these days when arriving somewhere for the first time, is no longer 'How are you doing' but 'What is the Wifi code'....

And let's not even start about the accidents caused by using the phone whilst driving. Horrific.

Lives, or precious moments of lives lost because of that wonderful invention called the smartphone.

And let's be honest, more or less every owner of a phone is guilty of the above. Some of it, or all of it. Just sometimes or frequently. I am guilty to it as well. And I just hate this stupid behaviour!

So, I can only come to one conclusion: the phone only becomes a SMARTphone when the owner knows when to put it down or switch it off.

Journaling "Smartphone"

How do I describe my relationship with my phone?

What parts of life am I missing because of my phone?

What's the wake-up call I need in this matter?

21 The curse of remembering

The other day I met this old man. He was just sitting there on the terrace and I happened to end up in a conversation with him. It took him only a couple of minutes to ask me if I knew his age. Of course I didn't but it was obvious he was proud of his years and after a clearly failed attempt to guess, he revealed his age; an impressive 102 years.

I love listening to these wonderful old people! They have seen so much, experienced so many things.

Just imagine: 2018 minus 102, so he was born in 1916. This Frenchman was born during the first world war and fought in the second, went through several economic crises, helped rebuild his country. And imagine all the things he must have experienced in his personal life…. There must have been lots of joy as that he must have experienced sickness and the loss of loved ones.

I saw a second ring on his finger and, sharp as he still was, he noticed that and answered the not posed question. He lost his wife three years ago and is wearing her wedding ring as a token of love. A tear came to his eyes and he shared he misses her every day. They've been together for almost 80 years….

"We had a good life" he said, *"but those damned Germans, who caused hell during these two wars, I will never forget nor will I forgive them"*.

His beautiful old face changed. It lost the glow of love and a mask of hatred and pain came over him. Instead of love, I could read the anger and the hate in his eyes. It gave me the shivers and made me sad.

He slowly turned around and pointed with his slightly bended finger towards the statue behind him. Like every French village or town, also here there is a statue to remember the loved ones they lost during the war. Mainly during the 'Grande guerre', the big war (WW1), they lost many but also the second world war caused lots of suffering.

"I lost my older brother in the first war and my younger brother in the second. And I still remember the German soldiers who took over our village. Who killed our fathers, brothers, our friends. Who slaughtered innocent woman and children, priests. I can still hear them shouting when they went from door to door searching for whomever they wanted to capture."

He kept talking and shared how he once decided to never forget, to never forgive his enemies and that for him the war would never be over. Because he would always remember.

It was as if I could feel his anger, his hate. His pain. His face dark, his eyes cold. His open hands turned into fists.

Because he once decided, all these years ago, to keep remembering, he never learned to see his former enemies as human beings. Because he decided to remember, he has nightmares every single night. The wars are over, yet he never found peace.

He became a prisoner of war since he could not forget, he could not let go.

When I walked away, I cried. For all the unnecessary suffering.

Journaling "The curse of remembering"

What do I need to forget, to release myself from the prison of my memory......?

Where did I harden my heart so I can't see those who once harmed me as human beings?

What would be the most courageous choice I need to make to let go of the past and embrace a life free of painful memories?

22 Guilty as charged

Nobody wants to hear that sentence. Except for a few 'special' people, even the biggest criminal doesn't want to hear this. When these words come out of the mouth of the judge, you're in trouble. Maybe you have to pay a fine. Maybe you even need to go to prison. And with that, something essential from you will be taken away; your freedom. Freedom to go where you want, to do what you want, even to be what you want. When the system works correctly, people are being sentenced to go to prison because they committed a rather big crime. According to the system, justice is supposed to be done and the offenders deserve it their freedom is taken from them for a certain amount of time. In the hope it'll correct them and that they won't do it again.

Recently I became more aware of a 'side job' I have taken on. It's a voluntary job and I'm afraid I must admit I didn't really study for it. Yet, I consider myself a specialist. Even much faster and more efficient than those who did study for it. I'm really good at it and it's no problem to do it whilst involved in other things. And really, I don't even want money for it since it comes effortless. It's as easy as breathing, really, I can do it 24/7. No prob! I'm always on duty and I just love it!

I am fully committed to this side job and it's like second nature, it just happens to me, whether I think about or not. I just love this self-appointed side job!!

Curious what it is? Let me tell you: "I am a judge". Yes, a judge and I'm a freaking specialist. In a split second I am able to charge and sentence people. I have this super-fast built in system that enables me to analyse, categorize, label, judge and sentence people. And they've committed serious crimes!! Really, they totally deserve my sentence.

Here are some of the crimes they committed: causing the traffic jam I am in, they are too thick, thin, tall or small. Dress horribly. Smell. Are too loud. Too silent. They are so arrogant or don't stand up for themselves. Block my view. Speak a language I don't understand. They look at me. Or not. There are too many of them. They together, me alone. They, they, they, the list of crimes is endless. It is so sad the world is so full of these kind of people. Luckily I am so wise I know why they are wrong....

And luckily I am not like them! Not at all! I am, well, maybe not perfect but at least I know the rules. If only everybody could be like me..... Luckily I am not like them, luckily I am not one of them. Just imagine.....

.......Sounds horrible, right.....? Shame on me!
I'm sure it isn't the same for you! Or maybe.... You do recognize something...?

We judge so lightly. We are prosecutor, judge and the executioner.
What happened to one of the wisest rule for life: *"Judge not, lest you be judged"*.

Journaling "Guilty as charged"

Where did I promote myself to a self-assigned judge?

Where would it be a good idea to look in the mirror before I judge someone else?

Where do I judge others to cover up my own offences?

23 Raison d'être

As a coach, I often hear people sharing they're not happy. Life is boring, their job is a pain. It just doesn't give them satisfaction and every working day they long for the weekend. Yet the weekend doesn't give the answer either. The next thing is an ongoing longing for retirement, not seldom dying from boredom shortly after.

A place with a rather different perspective on work, compared to most of the world, is Japan. Here is something funny, they don't even have a word in their language for retirement such as we know it in Western cultures. Japan also has the world's highest life span expectations, including high number of centennials. Next to an overall healthier lifestyle, most of the centennials keep themselves active, every single day.

What is it, that enables them to get up early every day to start their tasks with a happy heart and a smile on their face? No, money isn't the answer, nor is status. Yes, they get (financial) compensation for their work and they also are respected for it. But these are a side catch, not the driving force!

Their reason to get out of bed early isn't external, they found the driving force within themselves.

You're probably familiar with the experience that you, whilst doing something you totally love, completely loose sense of time. Your whole self is occupied with that one thing you're doing. As if you're in a state of trance. You become one with the activity such as the concert pianist becomes one with the grand piano. The only thing that can stop them playing, is the end of that piece of music. Not time nor tiredness. They're in an unstoppable flow whilst the music comes to life through them. Why can't artists stop creating, even when there's only little financial reward or recognition? Why is one person going to work with a huge smile on their face whilst the person next to them in the same traffic jam couldn't bother less?

Why do some of us really don't understand the concept of retirement?

The one thing they have in common is that they found their 'raison d'être'. Their reason for being, or as the Japanese call it, their Ikigai.

When we connect with the purpose of our life, when we consciously start bringing our activities in line with that, our work transforms into honouring our calling. Each moment we dedicate to that, is a joyful moment. Is a moment of flow. Where we forget about time, about the world around us. Yes, there will be obstacles to overcome, of course! Life will not just be a smooth ride to glory and success. But, as Nietzsche said: *"He who has a why to live for, can bear almost any how"*.

It is such a strong force of energy, impossible becomes an unacceptable word. There are even studies proving that survivors of the Nazi camps had one thing in common: a reason to live on the other side of the fence.

Our fences are often self-created.....My longing for you is that you find your reason(s) to climb and conquer these fences.

That you find your 'raison d'être'.

Journaling "Raison d'être"

What is the purpose I see for myself in life?

What are the fences I created between me and actually living that?

What is waiting for me on the other side of the fence?

24 Reasons to be

Congratulations! You've found your 'raison d'être', you know your purpose. You jump out of bed each morning and off to work with that huge smile on your face. You're the first to arrive, leaving last. The state of trance caught you and you're unstoppable. Fully focussed on that one thing that you decided to dedicate your life to.

One evening, whilst getting home late, your key doesn't fit in the lock. You look up to see if you're so confused that you're trying to open your neighbour's door. But no, it is your front door. You find an envelope taped to the door with your name on it. In it you find a note saying: "This key card is for the hotel room I booked for you. It seems all you need is a bed, a shower and room service. It's maybe the 'raison d'être' for the hotel staff to provide you that service, not mine." Signed, "your ex."

Everything in you resists the overwhelming message on this small piece of paper. You feel like shouting and banging on the door. Yet the energy for it is lacking. A deep tiredness fills you and all you can do is stumble back to the car.

You don't remember how you managed to get to the hotel. In the room you find suitcases with your clothes and boxes with personal belongings. In a corner your work related stuff. Your whole life, well, what's left of it, fits in one hotel room.

You look around realising it's true, indeed this seems to be all you need. A wave of sadness overwhelms you and you cry the most intense tears of your life.

With finding your calling, you lost your foundation....

The next morning, for the first time in years, you call in sick. Both surprised and worried your manager asks what's wrong? "Heartache", you answer.

It's true, your heart aches with the painful realisation you more or less forgot to live life whilst living your calling.

You once learned a tool called "Wheel of Life", an easy way to measure your levels of satisfaction for the key segments of life. You start drawing a circle, divide it in several wedges and you call it "My reasons to be". "I'm longing to be a good..." is your leading question.

Loving parent. Loving partner. Loyal friend. Dedicated professional. The first words come easy. But then it seems you have forgotten about life. You feel empty. It seems you only lived to work on your purpose and lost connection with the rest of life.

The rest of the day you draw one wheel after the other. After the first one you create specific wheels for each of the different segments. Asking yourself each time the same question: "What are the key ingredients of being a loving partner, parent, etcetera?" With each new layer of self-exploration and self-assessment the picture gets clearer and clearer: You destroyed the balance between your multiple 'raisons d'être'.

That evening, your partner finds an envelope on the front door. In it a note saying: "I turned blind but you opened my eyes. I would love to start over again. Included two tickets to the Virgin Islands".

Any alarm bells going off?

Journaling "Reasons to be"

Of what did I lose sight whilst pursuing my purpose or goals?

Of whom did I lose sight whilst pursuing my purpose or goals?

What is a healthy balance between my different 'raisons d'être'?

25 Who's the asshole?

Sometimes people surprise you. When you think you are good buddies you expect them to speak with respect about you. Well, actually, wouldn't it be nice you could always count on that? When you simply can trust there will be no talking behind your back. Of course we can do or say something that upsets the other and, when that happens, it would be awesome if the 'victim' gives you feedback on it. In private, at a carefully chosen moment. And, very important, in your face. That this person comes from "you probably just had a weak moment to do or say this and I'd like to share the impact it had on me". Where feedback is simply a gift coming from care and good intention. In that moment, on the receiving end, it might feel uncomfortable but shortly after you are grateful. For the honesty and courage. For the respect and good intention. And when we get over our ego, we're also probably able to look at the gift in that feedback. And the respect for the person giving this feedback, will only grow.

The other day I was surprised by someone I saw as a buddy, as my mate. We were on a trip with a bunch of guys where we shared highs and lows since, on such a trip, we frequently experience huge ups and deep lows. Often on the same day, in just a few hours, if not minutes. We joke about it, make a fool of each other, including ourselves. We live by Ben Zanders' "rule #6'; "Don't take yourself so damned serious"*.
You can count on it, this group of buddies won't let a chance pass to test if you can live by that rule. In order to create the space for a special vibe like that, above rule #6 is another one: we joke in your face, not behind your back. And when we give a punch, we are always ready to take one back.

One day, I heard one of the group broke the second rule and gossiped behind my back. Based on assumptions he spoke badly about me. He made me look like a total idiot without me being present. Not a smart thing to do, since the system always reveals its secrets. Middle aged men should know that by now. The code of trust was broken and the person who shared it with me also shared his worry: *"If he says this about you behind your back, what is being said about me when I'm not there"*?

And almost, almost I fell in the pitfall of responding on the spot. Say something like *"what an asshole"*. About the asshole, instead of to the asshole. I was disappointed by him talking behind my back and by me responding in the moment, I would have done the exact same thing. Just like that, without thinking.
Maybe all he did was the same thing. Just a slip of the tongue. So maybe he's not such an asshole after all. Would I have become the asshole making a big thing out of this....

Silence is golden. Time puts things in perspective.

*Reading tip: The Art of Possibility by Rosamund & Ben Zander

Journaling "Who's the asshole?"

Where am I making an asshole out of myself by my impulsive reactions?

What does it take from me to live by 'Rule #6'?

How am I with keeping silence?

26 Talent

They come in many different ways. Some are breathtaking, others are less impressive. Some are mind blowing, others are hilarious. Sometimes you wonder how on earth it's possible, sometimes you wonder what got into that person. Sometimes you can't believe nobody ever discovered this gifted person before, sometimes you hope somebody would have told them to try something else.

Some need a second chance, some steal your heart in seconds. Some make you laugh, some make you cry. Some are still very young, some are more senior. Some sing, some dance, comedy, fine arts, or not so artistic at all...

And it feels many more words are needed to capture the variety of people who come to one of these talent shows. Whether it is Britain, America or whichever country Got Talent, people just love participating in these shows. Some even fly all over the world to participate. The reason being, and it feels that they all have that in common, they want to bring a smile to our face or warm our heart.

Some are more experienced performing artists, not seldom it's the first time a participant is on stage.

Frequently the person on stage didn't sign up themselves, a loved one did it for them.

Where some are (very) convinced of their talent, others aren't at all. They shake and shiver, they giggle or can hardly speak. Sometimes I worry a bit and hope they won't faint from the stress they're experiencing.

Yet these are the participants I admire most! Imagine the courage it takes for them to walk on to that stage and stand in front of a critical jury and a huge audience. All the spotlights on them where they actually prefer to be hiding somewhere else. To me these participants are winners even before they even do anything. They've overcome a huge obstacle, the biggest obstacle between us and our success.

By walking onto that stage, they overcame themselves. Scared like hell, but they did it. They are champions because they've won one of the biggest battles we can fight in our lives; they've conquered their lack of self-trust and self-esteem. Their desire to share their talent with the world eventually got bigger than the monsters who tried to keep them hiding behind the curtains.

And when they open their mouth to start singing, frequently it is way beyond anyone would expect based on their entrance, based on their self-presentation. When they connect with that talent that lives in them, they transform from a shy child into a bright and shining star. It is as if another part of them takes over, the part that knowns and trusts. The part that totally believes in them; their inner power.

To them it is not about winning that show, they've already claimed victory.

Where in your life are you ready to claim victory? Like them, you may be too shy to become that champion.

The truth is, you already are. All it takes, is you stepping into it and own your talents.

Journaling "Talent"

Where do I need to claim victory before (or even without) going on stage?

What is the talent I'm hiding and long to embrace?

What do I choose to step into, or let go of, so I can let my star shine?

27 Enemies

It's a blessing to have some wonderful friends. Some of them I don't know not that long, others for decades. The record is more than 35 years! Travelling through life for so long with friends, you experience a lot, really a lot with each other. We've witnessed each other's marriages, held each other's new-borns. Held each other when we lost parents. Celebrated special occasions together and cried together when life was really tough. We've laughed our heads off and drank too much together. We worried over sickness and witnessed the suffering we all went through. We fought and made up. Spent holidays together, saw the kids growing up and becoming adults.

Well, I'm sure you know what I'm talking about....

Bottom-line is that I'm extremely grateful for having such people in my life and I pray we will grow much older together.

What is the opposite of a friend?

The obvious answer seems to be 'enemy'. I guess I don't consider many people as my enemy yet looking back in time, I can think of people who really tried hard to deserve this title.

One thing that really pisses me off is when someone constantly lies to me. Promises over and over, yet never delivering. An example coming up for me is when someone, after working a long time for this person, never paid for it yet over and over kept saying, next week, next month I'll pay. With each time a new excuse why not. It's not even so much about the money, yet the amount was substantial, but more about the constantly broken promises. At some point I really started to hate this person and I could no longer stand her presence. I was unable to forgive and it occupied my mind, better said, my spirit. After a long time of trying to find a solution, I finally understood it would never happen.

It was my birthday and I decided to give myself a huge and very expensive present: I sent a credit invoice and a note that I would close the file. It had to be over, I had to let go of this whole story, it drove me crazy!!

And, it feels I've learned something different about myself through this enemy, than I've ever learned about myself through my wonderful friends. Where my friends bring out the best in me, my enemy brought out my dark side. To the point it scared me. It shocked me which thoughts crossed my mind....

Looking back at it, I am grateful the universe sent this person on my path since there was a huge lesson I had to learn. I had to understand the dark side that lives in me. The devil that lives in me. That my ego can get so strong and stubborn that everything I think I stand for, gets thrown overboard.

The universe sent me this enemy to teach me a lesson, painful yet very important. Probably because I was so convinced about how right I was, I needed to be taught a lesson about how wrong I could be. I had to be sharpened. I had to be softened.

I so needed this teacher who 'dressed up' as my enemy.

Hmm, interesting concept....

Journaling "Enemies"

Who is my enemy who turns out to be my best teacher?

What is the lesson I needed to learn from this teacher?

How and where do I choose to apply this in my life?

28 Kids

"Daddy, do we have € 12.500 with us"?, Harry asked his father who stopped spontaneously because he was interested in buying a car from me. A question only a kid would ask with other people around. A totally logical question, and nothing wrong with it, but only a kid would say it. Right?

There is an endless list of things kids would say or ask that are so spot on, direct, transparent and shame-free which most adults would never dare to say that.

Kids are just very curious and simply ask what they would like to know more about, like: *"You have a weird nose, what is that spot on it"?* And whilst asking that question, preferably poke on your nose just to make sure it's clear it's your nose we're talking about......

Or when they hear a word they don't know, they just find out: *"Mam, what is a milf"?* Mother replies with a careful *"Well, just someone who is a really nice mother. Why"?* Her wonderful son answering with: *"Oh, John's father said you are a milf......"*.

Young kids do not know the word shame. They don't get the concept of 'politically correct'. They are so real and authentic, they simply say and ask anything that comes up. Frequently leading to hilarious situations for the adults who're neither the parents nor the 'victim'.

They just give words to what we all see, they are super straightforward with their feedback, they don't beat around the bush. It's probably something people dedicating their life to teaching small kids could write wonderful books about. An endless stream of funny quotes, 'inappropriate' questions and direct comments.

At least, that is how we adults see it, the kids are clueless about their unintended impact. They are so pure, what comes out of their mouth, even their non-verbal reactions is 100% about what they are experiencing in that very moment. And yes, they can cause awkward situations but they get away with it. What is it, that they can speak the hard truth, ask the weirdest questions and not get fired for it? Not end up in a fight or endless discussions?

To me it feels the main difference is that kids don't say these things with a bad intention. They are not smart enough, or is it mean enough to know how to set up a trap for someone. They just blurt what comes up since they are simply curious about what they observe. And when we, adults, take offence, it is our shame or our ego that gets in the way.

A sad milestone in a child's life is when they experience shame for the first time. That, until then, unknown feeling of unsafety, insecurity, self-doubt. It comes with a pain, that eventually grows so big, that we start to develop mechanisms to avoid this at all cost. The lying, manipulating, bending the truth and keeping up appearances begins....

Losing the child in us is one of the saddest moments in our life. Yet, I believe that we can all reconnect with this beautiful and pure energy that lives in us! This is unnecessary suffering...

What do we need to let go off to allow the inner child that's hiding in us, come to life again?

Imagine what it could bring if we would let go off the obstacles so we can allow the inner child that's hiding in us, come to life again?

Journaling "Kids"

Where in my life am I holding back because I feel I have to behave in a certain way?

What would it bring me, if I can be shame-free like an innocent child?

What do I choose to let go of to allow the inner child that's hiding in me, come to life again?

29 Right or Left?

Years ago I took the ferry to cross the North Sea between The Netherlands and England. It was a smooth journey and after a good night sleep in the cabin, we arrived. Everybody to their cars and I must admit, since it was the first time I would be driving in the UK, I was a bit nervous. I was used to driving on the right hand side, the Brits drive left. I slowly drove off the ferry and, simply following the other cars, I took the correct lane.

Shortly after I saw a sign that I found both hilarious as well as confusing. It said: ´Please drive on the right side of the road". And I am sure in this case, right was left.....

Playing with words is just funny, right?

And sometimes we catch ourselves playing with words in a not so funny way. I'm not even sure if we could call it 'playing' with words. We sometimes choose our words to convince people about us being right, to make sure they understand and admit they're wrong. We become a wordsmith, with a tongue sharp as a knife. We search for the weak spot to hit our opponent, after all, the aim is to get them on their knees.

Like a blacksmith we try to create the 'object' from iron or steel by forging that piece of metal, using all available tools to hammer, bend and cut it. For that we have to heat it to the point of melting, at least to make it flexible. We need to use force and hit it hard, or smart, as long as it bends into the shape we have in mind. The blacksmith does it to create something beautiful or functional from the metal he's working on. The force he's using is consciously yet with care and intention because his ultimate goal is to create something that is much better than the piece of metal he started with. Ever saw how a high quality knife is being made? It's a long process with many different steps. It requires patience and care. I would even say it needs a lot of dedication, respect and love for both the metal as the desired outcome, the knife, sharp as a razor blade.

The purpose of metal is to become some kind of functional object and for that it needs the will of the blacksmith to create it.

Human beings are not like a piece of metal that we can hammer, bend or cut until they get the shape we want them to have. A good discussion, great! Where you speak and listen. Where you are open for other perspectives, where you put your ego aside and are (wo)man enough to admit you were not (completely) right.

When you always want to be right, you will be left.....

So, maybe the question to chew on is, what needs to be left to be right?

Journaling "Right or Left?"

Where am I too stubborn to admit I might not be right?

Where is my tongue as sharp as a knife?

What is so important about being right?

30 Sexy

Let's admit it, we all have these moments when we see someone and we just can't stop watching. There is something about that person, the way s/he looks, walks, talks, is dressed, moves, smells, the look in their eyes.... whatever it is, there is a response in us where we all of a sudden become rather primitive creatures again.

Depending on the situation, maybe morals, maybe our courage we act upon it. Or not. Maybe we've learned how to behave properly (whatever that may be....) and we decide to close our eyes or look the other way. Or we don't want to upset our partner by openly staring and pretend we were looking at that nice car passing by. Or we say: *"Did you see that cute baby"?* Whilst in reality its sexy parent just took your breath away.....

Or these moments where your partner is not around and you feel there is a bit more room to flirt or maybe even play, also when realising it's like playing with fire. Yet the warmth of the fire is so attractive, you want to get close, closer, you might even find yourself on fire. Lust! Again, from totally well mannered, a correct, loyal, faithful and dedicated partner, it sometimes just takes one look that could transform you into a primitive 'hunter-gatherer'.

For a long time I thought it was just me. Boy, I felt bad....
Then I thought it was just men. At least it wasn't just me anymore....
In the meantime I've understood also women have a 'hunting-license' and suffer from the same thing. Well, suffer.....

Whilst not giving up on appreciating the visual impact someone sometimes has, there is something else that I find very, very sexy. Being a dedicated heterosexual this is something that can happen to me whilst looking at a woman as well as looking at man. There is something so sexy about that person, I just have to take another look. I really become curious about that person. I have to act upon it! It's like a magnet I can't resist.

This kind of sexy has nothing to do with that person's clothes, the way s/he walks or talks, nor have the looks of that person anything to do with it! There is nothing physical to this kind of sexy, it has nothing to do with sex! In the examples mentioned above, yes, I admit, it sometimes crosses my mind, but here, no, not at all!

This person is wearing the sexiest thing I can think of. It is so strong and convincing, you just want to be around that person. Not to watch nor to touch. Nothing like that!

You're captured by this person's energy and impact because this person is wearing the sexiest thing on earth: confidence.

When we trust ourselves enough to radiate confidence, we become a star and start shining. We become inspiring and magnetic. When we stop hiding behind our finger, when we give ourselves the courageous permission to manifest our inner beauty, we not only become the sexiest person on earth, we also inspire and encourage other people to do the same. What a gift!

How sexy do you dare to be?

Journaling "Sexy"

What do I really want to radiate?

What becomes visible when I stop hiding behind my finger?

How sexy do I really dare to be? Like, really......?

31 Parent or Partner

Sometimes I wonder when the first government decides that before we're allowed to become a parent, we need to take the 'School for Parents'. That only after successfully completing that program, having babies is legal. Of course it's totally absurd and from time to time as a parent I really could have done with it.....

For a wide selection of skills I have certificates and diplomas. Some were very useful, like Sunday school or swimming class, others were less useful, like math.

At Sunday school I learned stories and songs I could share when it was bedtime. Because I learned how to swim, we could go to Centerparcs or the Mediterranean where we had lots of fun!

But by the time the kids had math at school, I forgot all about it and the small bits I did remember, that's where they changed the way they do it. So totally useless!!

On top of that, by then I've been told 'leave me alone' a million times so even if I would have been a professor in math, it would have made no difference.

I don't know what it is they teach kids, somewhere during primary school, latest secondary school, they pick up something that fundamentally transforms your role as a parent. And this comes with little to no warning! Just like that they think they've grown bigger than their parents... And even if you would be warned, you wouldn't get it.

Looking back at it, the few warnings I got, came 'camouflaged' in the stories of friends complaining about their kids. They had become teenagers, a.k.a. temporary aliens.

What do you do?!? You let them vent, or cry, put an arm around them, tell them it'll pass. Well, pass it will for sure, the question is do we get what 'it' is?

The focus is on how to survive that new, really challenging behaviour of your teenager. Much less about what needs to shift in our behaviour in order to adjust to the upgraded demands of parenting. How wonderful it would have been to be a graduate from the 'School for Parents'! If only there would have been an outline how children's behaviour would evolve and giving us tools and tips how to adjust accordingly. How to play with the different shades of parenting. How to respond to all the stuff you'll be confronted with. One thing is guaranteed, the demands will evolve from caregiver and caretaker to helpdesk, safety-net and problem solver. You will have to deal with broken hearts, drugs, failed exams, alcohol, speeding tickets, lost jobs, getting arrested, etc. etc. Maybe not all of it but you'll get your share....

And at some point, they'll grow up. They'll find their own way. Did we as parents grow up with them without losing them on the way...? Did we learn and dare to let go and hold on at the same time.
The path from parent to partner is as fulfilling as it is very demanding, especially for single parents, most often single moms.
That school doesn't exist yet the world is full of teachers. All those who walked the path from parent to partner are qualified either by sharing their flaws or by sharing their successes.

How are you doing with letting go without letting down whilst walking the path from parent to partner?

Journaling "From parent to partner"

What does it take from me to grow up with my children?

What is my longing for the relationship with my children?

What does it mean to me, to be a partner for my children?

32 Embracing differences

Dare to be different! Be yourself! Well known statements nowadays and I love them!

For thousands of years people from so called "different" groups were not allowed to be themselves, yet the world finally starts to understand and slowly accept we all are different. We start to see being different is not a problem, not a disease, not something to be beaten out of people! On the contrary, it's a gift, it makes the world a more colourful place and a chance to create from.

It took long years of fighting, where countless people even gave their lives whilst taking a stand for their human rights. Correction, their lives were stolen from them by those who tried to force their will upon them....
The so called 'activists' had to fight for women's rights, gay rights, the rights of people whose skin doesn't happen to be white, religious rights, freedom of speech and so on. The list is endless.
The price was high. Gratitude and respect for all those freedom fighters!

Finally we can be who we are, say what we want. Be religious or not. Be gay or straight. You're free to openly choose where you feel you belong. To the right, to the left, in the middle, sometimes left, sometimes right. Both. None of it. Whatever you choose, wherever you position yourself, in general we can say, as long as you don't harm someone else, feel free to be and do as you like. Is the world finally growing towards being free from discrimination and indeed embracing differences? This would be such a blessing....

The last couple of years I see a shift that sometimes confuses me a bit. This is when we all have to be so equal, that differences are no longer acceptable. When those who say 'I disagree' are not accepted for having their different opinion.

I'm not (!) referring to people who hide behind their political, moral or religious (often limiting) beliefs and from there claim that something is wrong and that this gives them the right to make another person wrong. No, it are simply people who choose to live by certain standards and based on those standards they disagree with the standards other people live by. I see a shift that those who say 'ok for you, but not for me' become the rejected.

An example is where I see shop owners who refuse to be open on Sundays, now are being forced by law to open their doors that day. Or folks who really prefer to go to 'the ladies' or 'the gents', having to use the gender neutral (public) toilets.

Are we indeed moving towards 'embracing differences' or is the norm simply shifting?

It feels there is a problem embedded in the word 'different'. It includes we compare. And when human beings compare, they categorise and judge. Yes, we judge. All of us!

So here is a thought, instead of 'embracing differences', what about 'embracing uniqueness'? Where it is a human right to be unique which is what we are by nature. It's a given, just check your DNA.

Journaling "Embracing differences"

How are you uniquely different from others?

How do I want to be looked at, as different or as unique?

How do I choose to look at people, as different or as unique?

33 Rat race

Many books have been written on this topic. The famous rat race where people compete with each other. To be the first, the best, the fastest, the best paid, the....., well, the list is endless. To get to this point, we do a lot, including being less nice to the other rats. Like rats, we bite, fight, steel, anything to be at the front.

It's hard work, it's extremely tiring and not without risk. And when you finally find yourself in the front row of the group of running rats, it's even harder to also stay there. To keep your top position you need to fight a lot of opposition. Whilst you have to keep running fastest, and scanning all the obstacles on your path, you also need to have eyes in the back of your head. The other rats will do whatever it takes to make you stumble, and even better, make you fall. There is little to no mercy and it's usually a very lonely place where it feels you can't trust anyone.

We run, run, run......it's an endless race. Yet nothing but eternity is 'endless' so one day, one way or the other, the race will come to an end. We're overtaken and end up in the middle or even the back, we are being kicked out, fall sick or drop dead. Game over.

More and more of us start to see that and either decide to step out of the race themselves or never even start it. These are the smart ones, don't you think?

Human beings seem to be rather stubborn around the topic 'competition'. And I admit (most of this book is autobiographical after all....), I'm one of them. After stepping out of the rat race and starting my own company, a new kind of competition started. The competition of self-improvement. Self-growth is often seen as an ultimate thing we constantly need to strive for. We need to learn every day, become a bit better every week, beat the numbers of the same month a year ago. We start comparing ourselves with a competitor that never seems to let us of the hook: we're competing against our self. Another self-help book, another course, a seminar, a master. Whatever it takes to beat the current version of our self.

In our desire to be free from competition we actually started a competition that we'll never be able to win...... As the famous Dr. Seuss already wrote: *"There are games you can't win since you're playing against yourself...."*

Of course, there is nothing against growth! Yet I wonder what happened with the word 'enough'? What is so hard about accepting that what we have, that where we are, is enough? For a little while, maybe forever..
It seems we've replaced the rat race against others with the addiction to 'personal growth'. Personal and material growth. We're pushing ourselves for more, faster, bigger, better.... We push ourselves and we're very self-critical. Never enough, always better.
In other words, we find ourselves in a rat race with self......

We need moments to embrace 'enough'! To rest, reflect, celebrate. To consciously decide to either stay at 'enough', and trust that all you need is within you now, or to move towards 'more'. It's a balancing act.

Journaling "Rat Race"

Where am I in competition with myself?

What am I trying to prove?

What is the balance between 'more' and 'enough' for me.....?

34 A real man!

It is rather easy to figure out what a real man is. Just follow the commercials and let them tell you what clothes you should be wearing, how your hair should look like, a beard or not. What deodorant to use, how cool your car needs to be, how to show your muscles. How to walk, how to stand. How to talk and, for the post-modern man, how to cry.

Widen it to society and there are more patterns you could simply follow on your path to becoming a real man. It will inform you about which jobs are manlike, how to work your way up as man. How to be with other men, how to be with the ladies. The list of unwritten tips, advice and instructions is pretty long!

If you need more, just watch the movies! They'll spell it out for you! So many examples of real man are given, it's almost kind of stupid if you then still don't know!

Before writing this article, I googled 'real man'. The results are rather confusing! Instead of pictures of real men, Google Image mainly gave a series of quotes about how a real man is. A movie star with muscles as from steel shared his picture and next to it a one-liner that a real man should stand for his word and speak through his actions. Lots of quotes about how real men should behave. Many 'wise words' about how a man should be with a woman. One caught my eye. I guess it's aim was to underline that a real man accepts a woman how she is. A nice attempt yet maybe in essence still completely missing the point: "A real man never wants to change anything about a woman except her last name".

You are perfect as you are, I accept you as you are BUT all you need to change for me to marry you is your name. Your name?!? Our name is maybe the first word we recognize as a baby and maybe the last thing we can grasp when we grow really old. These few letters, in that unique order, forming your name is in a metaphoric way almost like your DNA. It's

YOU! A way of diminishing people is to constantly not call them by their name. To ignore that essential part of them.

I want to believe most men these days don't really buy the bullshit of commercials about what a real man is. I also want to believe most men these days are man enough to know how to be with a woman as well as with another man. That they know what it is to be human. Simply human. Correction, beautifully human.

Maybe a final step there is to let go of the old habit a woman has to change her name when she decides to marry a man.
To no longer force her to give up a huge part of a human's identity so a man can call her 'his'.
For a real man it's not in the name.....

Journaling "A real man!"

What is my take on 'a real man'?

Where do I put myself, or (other) men, in a harness of made up rules?

How is this question about what a real man is, important to me in the first place?

35 What a woman!

OK, after writing about a 'real man', it's only fair to also write about women. Yep, I understand, for a man this is a tricky thing to try.

I started the same way and used our wonderful 'resource of wisdom', Google. Hmmm, not sure if that was the best choice when I looked at what the first thing that came up told me: *"A real woman is a freak in bed, a chef in the kitchen, a therapist during hard times and a coach when you're off your game"*.

Seriously?!? Come on, it's the 21st century....

For the biggest part of history women have been seen as less than men, as the helper of men, as their pleasers. As not equal.

And sadly enough this is the case in many situations. It's unbelievable and unacceptable that women do not have equal rights as men. I leave out the word 'still' since it should never have been like this to start with! Men have used all kind of weird excuses to justify the way women were treated. Religion was, maybe still is, a favourite one. Or, also hilarious, that women would be not as intelligent as men. Or not as strong as men. Guys, we've got to get over all this bullshit!!

Throughout history women have proven to be as capable as men. Intellect and ability are NOT gender related! And the men who hold on to the last excuse of physical strength, well guys, try giving birth and then we'll talk again....

So far this seems to be a statement against the way women have been treated – and yes, I do take a stand against that! – and not so much about what a 'real woman' is. And I needed this introduction to get to this. Because to me it starts with seeing women as equal to be able to see a real women for who she is. It starts with not comparing! Not with men, not with other women. Comparing is competition and sooner or later that makes us a loser since we will always find someone who is better at something than we are.

So to me a real woman is a woman who dares to be who she is. To behave in the way she feels like. Who is not putting herself in the famous 'less than box', the place where we can feel sorry for ourselves for ever. Who is not putting herself in the famous 'better than box', the place where we can make a fool of ourselves for ever.

A real woman at the same time dares to be different! Yes, we are equal but thank God we're not all the same!! A real woman dares to express her uniqueness through how she talks, dresses, her work, through how and with whom she has sex with and you can add anything you like to this 'list of uniqueness'. Oh, now that the word 'sex' is out, for me the sexiest thing a woman can wear is self-confidence. That's when I say 'what a woman'....

My 500 words have been used, but I'm not done yet!

First, all what I've written above about a real woman, is also applicable to a real man.

Finally a question to the both genders:

Boys, what are your excuses to not take a stand against the differences?

Girls, what are your excuses to not take a stand against the differences?

Both of you, get over yourselves....

Journaling "What a woman!'

What is my take on 'a real woman'?

Where do I put myself, or (other) women, in a harness of made up rules?

How is this question about what a real woman is, important to me in the first place?

36 Sabbatical

As a frequent traveller I often hang out on airports. Waiting is boring so one starts looking around. Nice smells from restaurants invite me in to come and eat something. Not that I'm really hungry, but it kills some time. I'm rather conscious about my food, yet whilst traveling that's a challenge and I excuse myself with a 'hey, you're traveling, give yourself a break'. Instead of a small, I grant myself an extra-large cappuccino. That croissant looks yummy and I add it to the order. To find out they never taste as good as they look, let's forget it's even close to the croissants from bakery Le Fournil in my beloved Châtillon-en-Diois. After all, this is where the world's best croissants are being baked!
Hmm, shit, why did I do it again...?

After adding unnecessary calories to my diet, I take a walk to burn off a few. Bored as I am, I take a look at the duty free. Always something available I need. After-shave on sale, a perfume for the lady, and that wonderful headset is what I could really use. Frequent travellers deserve the luxury of good music! And thus I spend an impressive € 200 on freaking earplugs.
Hmm, shit, why did I do it? Again...?

I'm annoyed with my shopping behaviour so I decide to take a closer look at how my wife is misbehaving there. Makes a lot of sense! This way I can justify my own impulsive buying habits. Secondly, since money isn't an endless resource, I can rightfully ask her to shop less. After all she's spending a lot buying stuff on Amazon. She's not a frequent traveller as I am but wow, she's a talented shopper! Online is super easy and the 'magic plastic' always does the job! I start my investigations and easily find proof her online shopping is 'outrageous'. I put it on the table and depending on my mood I say it with love, or not so much love.....

Her response is great, she really tries to be more conscious and even checks if this month's budget leaves space for that purchase. My tactic works!

Another flight. Out of habit I walk into the duty free and start looking around. That battery pack is really cheap and great to have.

Then lightning hits me! What am I doing and who am I fooling here? How long will I blame my impulsive shopping on somebody else? What I'm doing is complete BS! It's me who's wasting money on stuff I don't really need and with that also harm the environment. I hate all the oversized packaging on small items yet I buy all that shit.

I complain for having to work hard to make the necessary money and envy those taking a sabbatical. On the spot I decide to take a sabbatical!

Not from working, from buying! From buying stuff I don't need. Clothes, a lot less, let me first wear what I have which is more than enough! Things? A hard stop! After hardly buying anything for more than a year, I discover I still have too much as it is. Re-using and decluttering is the new game. Less is more.

It's liberating. I love my work and don't really want a sabbatical from it. This 'buying-sabbatical' is awesome though! It doesn't only free-up budget to simply enjoy life more, also brain space.

What would such a sabbatical bring you?

Journaling "Sabbatical"

Where am I blaming others for behaviour in me that I dislike?

What does the word 'enough' mean to me?

What would buying less bring me?

37 Bullshit

Pardon my French! Yet sometimes that's the only way to describe something someone is saying. This person is saying things so negative, annoying, diminishing, destructive, below the belt, that it really hurts. Words have a huge impact. It hurts when someone hits you, it might make you bleed, leave bruises or maybe even scars on your skin. As a visible reminder of your attacker.

Though not visible, words can make you bleed as well. Words can make your heart bleed, can make your soul cry. They can bruise you and leave their marks. Permanent scars, sometimes even open wounds. Very, very painful to the point that they can leave a person limited or even handicapped for life.

These kind of words are total bullshit and should never be spoken. Yet I hear them often. It makes me sad, to the point of crying. Wondering if that person really isn't getting the impact of their words. Wondering how that person would respond if somebody else would be saying such words to them? Would they simply accept it, just swallow all that bullshit when somebody else would do this to them? Somebody else instead of them to themselves?

No, this not a typo. Many of us call ourselves names, say things about ourselves that are utterly mean and harmful. Hurting our own hearts with our own words, with a tongue sharp as a double edged sword. Cutting right through our soul.

I call this bullshit we dump on ourselves 'negativations'. Indeed, WORD gives a red line under this word, it's not mentioned in the dictionary. And I'm afraid it is so real to many of us – and to avoid using bad language all the time – that it deserves an official word. Negativations make us small, they lower our self-esteem, feed our limiting beliefs. They hinder us living our full potential and steal the courage to live our dreams away from us.

They serve no other purpose than shrinking us.

And why? Why on earth would we proclaim all this negative stuff over ourselves whilst we're born to manifest the glory of God that lives in us. To continue using the famous quote of Marianne Williamson, this is not just meant for some of us, no, for all of us! This powerful quote encourages us to embrace our talents, our brilliance. And since it seems we're more afraid of putting the spotlights on our magnificence than on our (so called) shortcomings, we deserve to bath ourselves in affirmations. Proclamations of self-worth. Balm to our soul.

It's a gift to be generous with compliments to others when we see them doing something well.

It's a gift to be generous with acknowledgments when we notice something inspiring in someone's being, in how they are. They make that person glow and grow.

In the same way it's a precious gift to self, as the antidote to negativations, when we are generous with affirmations. It'll make you glow and grow.

What is stopping you to be brilliant, gorgeous, talented, fabulous?

Journaling "Bullshit"

What are 'negativations' I am calling out over myself?

What of my wonderful self, my glory, is being suppressed by that?

What are some, at least 5, affirmations that I want to give to myself?

38 '24/7'

What?!? This WhatsApp is totally ridiculous! You are totally missing the point and I completely disagree! This really is against my beliefs, my standards. It's childish and just stupid! You are narrow minded and from another planet. It doesn't happen very often but this time I simply have to tell you you're wrong. And since I learned how to Swype, responding doesn't take much time. My beloved 'Swype-finger' dances over the screen of my phone and not long after I hit the 'send' button. Two grey check marks, message sent. There you go, soon you'll understand!
Two light blue check marks, message delivered and read.

Hmmm, what's taking him so long to respond? Too stubborn to admit he's wrong?
Still nothing. Annoying. I can see he was just online, what's going on? Did I piss him off? Is he…..? Will he…..? All kind of scenarios start crossing my mind, none of them are actually uplifting.

After almost a day, which feels like an eternity, my screen tells me there is an unread message. It's him. He needs a lot less words than I did. The message is short and simple. Unlike mine, not charged, not sharp. Not trying to convince me. All it says is: "We seem to have a different take on this my friend. When do meet again for a drink? Miss you!"

What?!? What? What……am I missing here? Slowly it occurs to me that I might be the one who's missing the point. The point is not who's right or wrong. The point is not who has the best arguments to convince the other. The point is not who will win.
The point is who's willing to listen. Not only with his ears, also with his heart.

The point is who's willing to not only hear, but also to understand.

The point is who's wise enough to self-manage impulses and not over shout the other.

The point is who's warm and courageous enough to listen through a filter of love, filtering out what's not growing the relationship.

The point is who is smart enough to look at everything from at least 7 different perspectives. Seven different points of view on the same thing. If still attached to the words right and wrong, there is right and wrong in everything. There is your truth, there is somebody else's truth. There are your circumstances as well as the other person's circumstances. Your shoes, his shoes. And so on. There is very little black and white in life, everything deserves to be explored for its shades and colours.

Yes, this takes time! Actually, this gives time. Precious time. Time to get over yourself, to not give in to your impulses. We can start a fight in one WhatsApp, a war in 140 characters.

My dream is that I, that we, all people, which includes presidents and kings, learn to give our response a 24/7. No, that doesn't mean we're always and immediately ready to respond to everything!

This 24/7 gives us 24 hours of reflection and 7 perspectives to be explored before responding.

Journaling "24/7"

What is the price I am paying for responding without giving it time for reflection?

What is so important to me about making my point?

What / who could help me to explore different perspectives?

39 Self-care

Taking really good care of ourselves becomes more and more acceptable. Not that long ago self-care was perceived as 'self-ish', yet nowadays we get encouraged to take really good care of ourselves. Get enough sleep, eat well, relax, avoid stress, enough vacations, exercise, a massage maybe? Get a dog and take it out for walks. Meditate, do yoga. Go on a silence-retreat. Take time off from running the household and the kids, you're entitled to have you-time!! We need to live by the 'oxygen mask-principle': take care of yourself before you take care of others. This isn't a luxury, it's a necessity! Without this life is not sustainable and all kind of health threats, like a burn-out, might be knocking on our door.

Marinate self-care in self-love and you're on your way to nirvana. Self-love. Instead of 'love your neighbour as you love yourself' we now say 'love yourself as you love your neighbour' since we've been trained to respect and care for others so well, that we frequently care more for others than we care for, than we love ourselves. No, not a good idea!

The concept is clear. Taking care of yourself is now more or less a right of the post-modern human being.

Do you feel the 'but' coming? Or as coaches like to say, the 'yes, and'? There is indeed a poison that keeps us from experiencing heaven on earth. From a heart at peace, a soul that doesn't know pain, a mind without worry. Sometimes in ignorance, though often by choice we drink that poison. Maybe it's because this poison has no taste nor smell so that we believe we can consume it without experiencing any consequences. We actually believe there is something special about this poison. We drink it yet expect somebody else to die from it. Hmm, interesting concept.

Initially that seems true indeed. Yet sooner or later we start feeling slightly unwell. We sleep less, feel somewhat restless. We experience anxiety or headaches. Our mood changes, some start feeling depressed. We're clueless why, even the doctor can't find clear reasons. But the symptoms become stronger and stronger, we need help!

On a good day you meet an angel in your dreams who asks you why you keep drinking poison? *"Which poison"?*, you respond. *"The one that holds you back from forgiving this person who harmed you"*.
In your dream you have an intense conversation why this person does not deserve your forgiveness.
Then the angel puts her hands around your heart. *"What do you do"?* you ask, whilst you feel something shifting deep inside you. *"I'm softening your heart"*, the angel says.
"Your heart needs to soften to stop the suffering. You're suffering because you don't forgive. You're punishing yourself because you can't forgive."

You really long to be free from this pain but your heart is too stubborn. You ask: *"How? What should I do"?*
"You need to add one thing to your self-care skills", the angel answers. *"Learn how to forgive and let go"*.
All it takes is a choice. A choice to love yourself so much that you forgive the other.

Are you willing to make this ultimate choice of self-care?

Journaling "Self-Care"

What is the poison I am drinking?

Where am I unwilling to forgive others?

Where am I unwilling to forgive myself?

40 The Big Bang

There is something interesting about our relationship with emotions. Pretty soon in life we start teaching our children how they should express their emotions. When they are sad and cry, we comfort them and whilst doing so we tell them to stop crying. As if crying is a bad thing.

When they get angry, we tell them to behave, be mindful of their language, to suppress their anger as soon as possible. As if being angry is a bad thing.

When they laugh too loud, we tell them to quiet down. To 'do normal' again. Whatever 'normal' is, as long as it is not that loud, which might upset other people. As if laughing out loud is a bad thing.

More examples can be given, the picture is clear; expressing our emotions is in many parts of the world not really acceptable.

Of course intellectually we understand it's not very healthy to not express emotions but the social norm seems to be more important. Expressing emotions often is seen as losing control and being vulnerable, weak even. Evolution taught us the weak ones die first, so we avoid being perceived as weak at all cost. Keeping up appearances wins!

In the meantime we also know that with suppressing emotions they are not gone. It can feel like a balloon to which we keep adding air. For a long time it seems the balloon just gets nicer because it grows and grows. And then, with that tiny bit of additional air, which in itself is nothing, the balloon explodes. The big bang! The individual felt it coming but the outside world is surprised and often rather judgmental that such a small thing made the individual (over)react so strongly.

Something 'funny' is happening simultaneously. We don't dare to express our emotions and feel horrible about that, yet at the same time we seem to treasure them. Let's take an emotion like anger as an example. Something happens, someone does or does not do something that upsets us and we get angry. Very often not expressed or not expressed fully and the anger stays in our 'emotional balloon'.

Next to expressing an emotion and share it with the world around us, we can also choose to just let it go. Pull up your shoulders and let it go. Somebody once said "emotions last only 7 seconds, after that it becomes a choice". Forget about the number of seconds, the choice-part feels very true. We can choose to let go, forgive, not make it so important, not make ourselves so important, try to see it through the eyes of the wrongdoer. Whatever works best for us at that moment, we have tons of tools to pick from to make a conscious choice and deflate the balloon. By allowing the compressed air from the balloon to be released into the endless space of the oxygen around us, we harm nobody yet we heal ourselves.

Emotions, express and let go. The big bang is a choice.

Journaling "The Big Bang"

What is my perspective on emotions?

What is the price I am paying for not expressing my emotions?

What does it take, to deflate my balloon?

41 Love, a radical act

Love, one of the most used words in the world. It's hard to imagine a single person in the world who doesn't know the word. It's the most popular theme for songs, books and movies. Let's not even try to count how many dreams mankind had with love as the main theme. Nor can I remember anyone ever saying they don't need or want love. Love is a basic human need.

Love is expressed and experienced in many different ways. Romantic love, the love for our children, between friends, in our families and communities. Our pets.

Love is a basic human need and yet, do we dare to live that human need? We long for it, we strive for it, we play with it. We do everything for love. And when it comes to it, do we dare to admit it, to say it? Or when we finally have the courage to do so, we're maybe afraid of the consequences. A famous love song, performed by Frank Sinatra says:
"The time is right, your perfume fills my head, the stars get red and, oh, the night's so blue
And then I go and spoil it all by sayin' something stupid like "I love you"….

These three words, "I love you", a basic human need, spoils it all?
What are we afraid of? Rejection? Finding it and losing it again? Somebody's disapproval to love someone or something?
If we don't dare to love out of fear of losing it again, we don't dare to accept our human need. We're stealing away essential food from our heart. It's the same as if we would constantly not take in enough food to keep our body functioning. Kind of silly, isn't it?

If we don't dare to love because we're afraid how another loved one feels about that, hmm, is that real love? As Sting sings, 'if you love someone, set them free'. I assume 'free' includes the freedom to love. OK, loving kids and pets usually isn't perceived as threatening. But how do you feel when your partner says "I love you" to another man or woman?

Love is a radical act. Radical isn't just rebellious and loud. Radical is something that comes from your core, from your inner roots, your essence. Radical also includes changing views and habits. When expressing your love - and let's not confuse love with sex –as a radical and authentic act, it's a precious gift.
Sorry mr. Sinatra, we don't spoil anything, it's not stupid at all!
I'm totally hetero yet really OK to say "I love you" to my gay friends, to any other man.
I'm committed to my marriage and I feel free to say "I love you" to another woman.
Nothing and nobody has an exclusive right to your love. When we dare to proclaim we love someone, the world becomes a better place since we can't really love someone and harm that person at the same time. Love is an abundant and self-multiplying emotion. The question is, do you dare to love and do you dare to express it? Or is it easier or more acceptable to say 'I hate you?

And, do you dare to allow your loved one to love someone else?
Maybe an interesting conversation to have......

Journaling "Love, a radical act"

Where in my life am I being stingy in showing or giving love?

What is exclusive to me about the words "I love you"?

What does radical, coming from my core, mean to me with regards to love?

42 Just a bridge

Many of us ask ourselves wonderful questions about why we exist. We can spend a lot of time, sometimes our whole life to find an answer to this. Maybe we never get really satisfied with the words we find or we keep reshaping them.

It's indeed a huge and very important question to answer. Maybe it's a question that even doesn't want to be answered. Perhaps it is a question to always struggle with and never be satisfied with the words. Not for a long time at least. It could be that we experience a certain peace with the words we find at some point, but life moves on and so do we.

The words are like the shell of a lobster. As long as we keep growing into our shell, it's all fine. It holds and protects us. Like the shell, words don't grow. At some point, when the shell gets too small for the lobster, it has to shed it. In order to grow, it has to leave the safety of that shell and inhabit a new one. If it won't, the lobster will eventually kill itself, simply by growing. So potential needs space.

At some point we will outgrow the words we found for the reason of our existence and we need to shed them. We need to leave the comfort of those words and struggle for a while, until we find new ones. Whilst they grow on us. Only then we feel comfortable again.

My longing for everyone is indeed that we experience a lifelong struggle with these words, with the essence of why we exist. It'll support us to live a life on purpose, to blossom and bear fruit.

At the same time, the risk of this is that we start feeling that we're pretty important. That we get so focussed on what our purpose is and how to express it, that we forget we are just one small individual in a countless series of generations. One day we will have to leave this world and this body to become one of the stars. We will be just a little sparkle of light in an endless galaxy. A dot, nothing more than a dot.

As kids do in their sketchbooks, we also connect the dots in the sky and we start seeing figures.

I like to see this as a metaphor for how we can connect the dots between the generations. My great-grandparents are dots in the sky. All the generations before them. All the generations after them and I'm just one of them.

Before I become such a dot, I'd like to see myself as a bridge. I am nothing but a bridge who's connecting the previous generations with the next. That's all. It's maybe not even that important what kind of a bridge we are. A simple plank over a tiny little stream or a huge one crossing a sea?

So, if I am not that important since all I'll become at some point is a little star in the skies, maybe I might as well live by Rule #6 presented by Ben Zander in the book 'The Art of Possibility: Don't take yourself so g-damned seriously.

Make the most of your life, and….. chill…..

Journaling "Just a bridge"

What kind of a bridge between the generations do I long to be?

Where am I creating a shadow to avoid my star to shine its light on the world?

What is important to me about 'shining my light' on the world?

43 Fierce Courage

"A Catholic, a Jew, a Protestant and a Muslim get together to discuss some of the bigger questions in life. One starts with sharing his sins. The others look at him and think….."

This sounds like the beginning of a good joke, right? With an unexpected, sharp and funny ending, often with some kind of deeper message hidden in it. At first it confuses you, then it humours you, eventually it teaches you. The power of great jokes.

What I experienced wasn't a joke.

A Catholic, a Jew, a Protestant and a Muslim were indeed discussing some of the bigger questions in life. And as soon as one started sharing his 'sins', the others looked and him and thought, shit, this is courageous of you to share this! Probably, no, for sure, if you would take the Bible, the Torah and the Quran, all of them would have labelled these acts or thoughts as sins.

Then the next one shared. And the next one. And the next. All four spoke freely about something where we felt our actions or thoughts were not in line with our religious or cultural backgrounds.

We had this conversation during a leadership programme and of course we discovered the hardest person to lead is ourselves. The programme predicted that and gave us an exercise to explore the multiple facets of our inner diamond. What becomes available when light shines on all these facets of your inner beauty? We had a wonderful visualisation to prepare us as well as some great homework questions to evoke some powerful insights.

A bit shy, all confessed the visualisation didn't really work for them nor did we do the homework.

Instead we did 'heart-work'. No, we didn't explore what makes our heart beat faster or what makes it even jump from joy. There was something else to be explored first. The stuff that makes our heart feel small, shy, ashamed. The stuff that we'd rather keep secret, that we do not even dare to commit to ourselves. We explored our shadows, our dark sides. Not just 50 shades of grey, no 50 shades of black.

Wow, how liberating that we could share this freely, in a place without judgement. Instead we experienced recognition and acceptance. If the programme would have ended here, it would have been a blessing already.

There was more. One of us was a huge step ahead of the rest. Where you think it is courageous to share this kind of stuff with a bunch of strangers, it becomes fierce courage when you can share these things with your partner. This is what I've done, this is what I long for. It might be against the norm or another rule, and still, this is who I am, what I want. I love you enough to trust you with my dark side. I need to come clean with my dark side and I hope you will still be able to love me when I do. And I'm willing to pay the ultimate prize if you can't. I can't lie to myself nor do I want to lie to you.

In awe we gazed at this person. You powerhouse. You role model of fierce, authentic courage. From self-acceptance to self-authority. Radical. From the core.

When lying to yourself is no longer an option, you've found a new level of freedom.

Journaling "Fierce Courage"

What's the 'heart-work' I need to do?

What's the conversation I need to have, with myself or anyone else to get to the next level of freedom?

What's the lie I can no longer live?

44 Just 250 grams

We're wasting every single day. We're wasting time, chances, money, the moment to speak. We're wasting the opportunity to tell someone you love her or him. The chance to give a hug. To smile at someone. To enjoy life. And, let me not forget I'm a coach, we're wasting our potential.

No, I'm not in a grumpy mood yet this is probably one of the most grumpy chapters in this book. No complaints afterwards, you're warned so if you decide to continue reading, it's your own choice.

I'm not grumpy, I'm angry. Yes, angry! All the wasting listed above, most of it is 'just' your loss. Too bad. Get over yourself, get a coach, do nothing, whatever, it's your life.

What I am angry about is the way we waste our planet. What got into us that we have to send ships out on the ocean to clean up plastics islands floating out there. Who the hell do we think we are we can use this planet, correction, abuse this planet as if we're the last ones living on it?!?

We're spraying poison on our food thinking that's a good idea. It's fucked up!

We're making our cars 'green', yet we do nothing about all these huge tankers crossing our oceans who burn the most dirty oil you can imagine. It's fucked up!

We're wrapping food and items in pointless amounts of plastic. It's fucked up!

We're accepting plastic bags without a single thought about the consequences. It's fucked up!

We're buying things we don't really need and throw them away after we get bored with them. It's fucked up!

We are just a single generation who's borrowing this planet from the next generation. From our children and grandchildren.

We've got a poster in our house with all kind of smart-ass quotes and one of them says 'leave everything a little bit better than you've found it'.

Let's do a little math, just for fun. We've got 7.6 billion people in the world. Let's say each person creates just 250 grams of waste per day. That's not much, right?

WRONG! Put it on a pile and you get a mountain of 1.900.000.000 kilo of waste. Clueless how much that is? Assume a car weighs 1.500 kilo's, that makes a traffic jam of like 1.25 million cars. That's like 7.500 - 10.000 kilometres. Get the picture? It is fucked up!

This is why I am angry. And sad. And lost because I don't know how to solve this huge problem.

The thing is, I'm also guilty. I'm contributing to this huge mountain of waste. The visible and invisible waste I'm creating. I'm as guilty as you are. So I'm also angry with myself, as much as I'm angry with you and the rest of the world's population who's robbing this planet from future generations.

I really don't know how to solve this yet I know I can do something. I can change my habits.

It probably starts with saying 'no' more often. 'No' to that plastic bag. 'No' to products and food wrapped in silly amounts of plastic. 'No' to buying stuff I don't really need.

Another step is saying 'yes' more often. 'Yes' to every child I see, promising them I'll do my utmost to leave this planet a bit better than I found it. That I'll do what I can to give them a liveable place.

Probably you're not as bad as I am, and still, what about your 250 grams?

Journaling "Just 250 grams"

How do I want to leave this planet for the next generations?

For this, what am willing to say 'yes' to?

For this, what am willing to say 'no' to?

45 To see or not to see

"How are you doing"?

Four words. Just four very simple words. Asked whilst coming from a sincere curiosity.

The "How are you doing" was initially answered with a question mark in her eyes. As if she was really surprised. Surprised that somebody asked her how she's doing. Asked her, of all people. The one who stands out in the group, not for how visible and talkative she is, but for her highly developed talent to be quiet and listen. Where others express their excitement and involvement with words, she usually only speaks when explicitly asked. And even then the words are limited and carefully chosen. Spoken with a soft voice. Gentle and soft. Often it's been so long since she last spoke that she needs to scrape her dry throat a little bit. The words coming out of her mouth are so soft that you need to listen carefully to hear them.

Yet, the listening is totally worth it. The more verbal ones in the group may already be speaking again, and with that missing the gift in the words she shares. Where the words of the louder ones sometimes only feel as if they are just moving air, the words coming from her mouth are in general meaningful and rich.

But this reflection is not about who is saying the smartest things. This is not even about consciously spreading out the airtime people get more equally. We're all communicating in our unique way and that's absolutely fine. And in all honesty, I don't even really care; I'm a trainer in coaching, not a Toastmaster!....

What I do care about though, is that people feel seen and respected for who they are. We confuse being more talkative with being more important, interesting, maybe even more intelligent. Maybe with being more worthy even.....?
We confuse being less talkative with being less interesting, important or less smart. Less worthy?
Huge mistake!

This often starts at a rather young age, like at primary school where the introverts are being labelled. Labelled as what? Well, fill in the blanks yourself. Labelled by the system, by extroverts, maybe by other introverts, or even by themselves.

Or does it even start with using words like introvert and extrovert.......?

Every label that comes with judgement or assumption has the potential to hurt the other human being. Putting people in a box is narrow-minded and often just caused by the insecurity from the one who invents the box....

Whatever 'vert' we are, in essence we all can do without that shit. Really!
Instead, we simply want to be seen and heard. For who we are at our core. For our true self.

Often all it takes are four simple, yet genuine words; asking that other human being "How are you doing."

Journaling "To see or not to see"

Who do I give more attention, introverts or extraverts?

Where am I speaking more than my words deserve?

Where am I speaking less than my words deserve?

46 The generosity of the candle

Probably without being very aware of it, we spend a lot of time comparing ourselves with other people. We look if they make more money, have a bigger house or car. How often they have a holiday and how expensive that might be. We look at the job they have, the clothes they wear. The street they live in, the friends they have, the family background. We look at their hobbies and how good they are at sports. How cool their dance moves are. At how smart and well behaving their kids are. How sexy their partner is, how sexy they are.

We compare and compare, endless comparing....

The funny thing is that we are very selective with whom we compare and with which parts of that person. We hardly ever compare ourselves with 'the average person' whilst looking at the complete picture of that average person's life.

I guess this is how it more or less goes,: We find something in ourselves where we're unhappy, let's say our job. Nah, too boring, let's do how sexy we are. We then choose somebody whom we find more sexy than our self. Great, now we can feel even more shitty about ourselves because we can put 'poor me' in the 'worse than' box.

At the same time we filter out everything else of that person that isn't better than how we score ourselves on these points. That they can't tell you the sum of 2 + 2 is irrelevant, since they have a sexier body. No, we don't look at the complete picture, we choose selectively, we choose to lose.

So, we often compare to make ourselves feel less; kind of silly, isn't it...

The game of comparing is actually one big competition. We constantly compete with the whole world. It is an endless game since we can always find someone who is better at something than we are. We are in a game we can never win. Maybe on one or a few parts, but the whole game. Nah, never!!

Playing a game you can never win, is setting yourself up for trouble.
I'm convinced that's not why we're on this planet. A bit of healthy competition, such as in sports or games, fine, enjoy it! For the bigger picture of our lives, I wholeheartedly believe we are meant to support each other by adding our talents to the talents of the other person. There is something where you excel, there is something where you are less talented. This is the same for everyone! So get over yourself and stop competing, start completing. Complete the other where they need your talents. Allow the other to complete you where you need their talents. There is so much joy and fulfilment in multiplying by sharing! When you share your talents you will create synergy, this is how 1 plus 1 equals three.
Do it like the generous candle who lights another candle. A candle doesn't lose anything by setting another on fire. For a brief, almost intimate moment they share the available oxygen and then both can burn freely and together they multiply the light and warmth.
As long as you have your light shining, you can be endlessly generous and light thousands and thousands of candles.

And, did you ever see a candle comparing itself with another candle and wonder if their flame was good enough.....?

Journaling "The generosity of the candle"

Where do I no longer want to compete and do I, instead, choose to complete?

How do I light other candles?

What are my gifts and talents I choose to share generously?

47 Don't worry, be free

There is a woman that I admire and love a lot. The main expression on her face is a warm smile. Love in her eyes when she looks at me. There are tears in her eyes when I suffer. An open heart when I need more love. She's a great listener. Fast to accept, slow to judge.

She also has a great lesson for people who struggle, potentially for no reason. It's just a simple saying, yet so deep and often painfully true.
I've heard her say this frequently, for as long as we know each other. That's for as long as I live since this woman, is my mother.
My mother, now 85, so often shifted perspective with her saying 'a man suffers most from the evil he fears'.

Fears. I've had many. Evil fears. I have had sleepless nights because of them. A huge part of these fears has been around my son. Over the years they grew bigger. From rather innocent ones, like will he find his way to school alone. As soon as the word 'safely' was added to this sentence, the fear became more evil....
With him growing up, the fears grew. Like when I found that first liquor bottle under his bed. When I couldn't trust anymore if he would not drink and drive.

It found its climax when drugs and alcohol took over his life. At some point I prepared myself for the worst case scenario. When I didn't expect anyone to ring the doorbell, in a split second a terrifying thought formed...."would it be the police...?" Or when my cell phone showed an unknown number. I died many deaths fearing these fears..... Were these thoughts stupid thoughts? Maybe not, maybe they were. Yet this is not the question! The real question is what was I doing to myself by the emotional charge I gave to these thoughts. I was suffering because of what I made of the doorbell or my phone ringing. That was just a sound with a simple meaning: somebody wants to me to open the door or somebody wants to talk to me. It was me who translated this into 'the police is coming to tell me my child died'.

I forgot the lesson in my mother's words. I was suffering most because of the evil I feared. I'm convinced it didn't make me a better father either.... I was actually adding to the mess because my fear paralysed me. It stole my own spiritual freedom as well as from the freedom to take a stand against the things I saw unfolding in my son's life. It stole away the courage to fight against the addiction, whilst still loving the addict.

This is just one of the examples in my life, where I forgot about my mom's wise words. Fear kept me in relationships where I should have stepped out. In jobs I should have quit. It stopped me from saying I love you where I wanted to. It kept me from going for that dream, from taking that risk. Oh yes, in more than half a century I added quite a bit to my own suffering and with that, stole away from my freedom to live without worry.

Give it some thought where your fears paralyse you to think and to live freely? Where are you adding to your own suffering, or even creating it? Because really, my mom has a point....

Journaling "Don't worry, be free"

What made up fear am I suffering from?

What do I worry about that amplifies my fear?

What do I choose to lean into to release me from my fear?

48 Providence

Driving home during the night. It must have been around 2AM. Not much traffic on the road anymore and all service stations already closed. It had been a long day and I was really longing for my bed and tried everything to not fall asleep. Singing loudly along with the music. Despite the cold I even opened my window to get a breeze of fresh air. Luckily, the next exit was mine. Almost there.

Then it happened! That moment of relaxing into the 'almost there' made me close my eyes for a moment. Without realising it I drifted asleep, heading towards a huge accident.

Yet there was something that corrected my destiny......It felt as if there was a big hand that picked up my car, put it back on the road and woke me up. This body wasn't ready yet to leave this world. There was something not complete in this life.

If this may sound woo woo to you, a little crazy even, I'm with you. I mean, I was.
In at least four different situations my life was in immediate danger and I got out of all without even a scratch. Three times in traffic, once I almost drowned. On my way to leave this life and each time there was this miraculous force that decided otherwise.
What is that about? What is that force? Do I have a guardian angel or another higher power taking care of me? Is this the hand of God? I don't know nor do I really need to know or understand. It is clear to me there is something bigger than I am out there that has a say in my destiny.

I started to observe how many things happened to me or other people around me where we could say "this is coincidence". After taking a closer look, in most cases, actually in all of them, the conclusion could only be that coincidence still doesn't exist.

If coincidence does not exist, these events must happen accordingly to some kind of plan or conscious choice. And since that plan or choice is clearly not ours, who or what is then responsible for it?

As H.W. Murray writes in one his famous quotes, when we commit to something, Providence moves and a stream of unforeseen events occur. Providence; according to the Cambridge dictionary, is 'an influence that isn't human in origin'. The Oxford Dictionary describes it as 'the protective care of God or of nature as a spiritual power, timely preparation for future events'.

Maybe it then was Providence that decided my life wasn't complete yet. I'm not the kind of man who really understand these big things. Maybe nobody really does. Yet I am convinced that influences from another dimension are waiting to partner up with us. To protect, to guide, to inspire. They'll always be there and I do believe this is something that goes above and beyond religions, perhaps they're even the binding factor between religions. Maybe that's why it's called spirituality and not religion.

Whatever you want to call it, that's fine. You're encouraged to find your way, your relationship with the things that seem to be from another dimension.

Maybe there is no scientific evidence for Providence, yet what do you make out of all these things that are beyond logic and reason.....?

Journaling "Providence"

Where were things in my life too much coincidence to not believe they were meant to be?

What is my relationship with Providence?

What does it take to let the desire for 'logic' explanations go and lean into so called coincidence?

49 Taking a stand

Teaching other coaches the profession, takes me all over the world. This may sound all really cool, the reality is far less romantic and exciting. Spending time on all these airports isn't the most exciting thing, nor are cancelled flights. What comes with hanging out on airports, is that you get to see people's dark side. When people travel, they are frequently somewhat nervous which makes them act different from usual. Long flights often make people tired and tiredness easily makes people grumpy and irritated.

I'm convinced stand-up comedians can find lots of material for their shows at airports!

So do writers!

November 2018, Boston airport. After we got boarded for the flight to Amsterdam, the machine had a technical problem that couldn't be fixed and the flight got cancelled. I can tell you, that news didn't put a smile on my face.....

After a 24 hours delay we tried again and just before boarding I went for a little bite to a small airport bistro, where I knew both the food and the service were nice. After ordering with Casey, the waitress, I looked around and noticed some people making a huge mess. Food and spilled drinks all over the place. Of course, shit happens, yet no need to act as if nothing happened and not take the smallest initiative to get the mess cleaned up. You know, what would you do at home? Clean it up, right? So why not when this happens in an airport restaurant?

At that moment Casey came with my order and I saw she noticed the same situation. Our eyes met and we knew we were thinking the same. I noticed a sigh escaping her mouth but that was the only way she expressed her frustration. When she put my order on the table, I said something like 'that sucks' and she nodded a subtle yes. I asked her *"If we agree to keep it our little secret, what is it that you would say"*?

Her reply was a big lesson to me. Where I became judgemental, she made another choice. Casey told me she's been working on the airport for like 10 years now and yes, people's behaviour changed. So it didn't get easier. But she wanted to hold on to the lessons her grandparents, who raised her, taught her. Casey was taking a stand for good old basic rules of life, such as respect. *"Sir"*, she said, *"if I would lose my temper, I would become the same as the people whose behaviour I disapprove. I choose to not go there and rather focus on doing my job as good as possible. And I hope that people will notice and be inspired by it."*

Casey, you're saying something very important here! When we think we can change jerks by becoming a jerk, we miss the point. Looking at your age and knowing how long you work here, you've probably left school rather young yet you hold a wisdom that's beyond degrees and titles.

You taking a stand in silence makes it even more powerful! You are showing a powerful form of leadership: by example!

I'm grateful for meeting Casey. You gave important questions to chew on.....

Journaling "Taking stand"

Where can I take a stand without picking up a fight?

Where do I become a 'jerk' trying to correct other jerks?

Where can I lead by example and be the change I want to see in the world?

50 Border Collie Syndrome

The old scriptures of the Bible hold a very special command. Not a command to do something or to not do something. This command is not forbidding anything. This command is not forcing anything upon anyone. It is a command that doesn't want to limit in any way shape or form. It is an ultimate example of equality and sharing. This command, when honoured to its intention, can't harm anyone. This command doesn't make anyone pay taxes, nor does it hinder anyone in their freedom. When this command would be respected all over the world, war would no longer exist. It comes for free and you can only gain.

Curious? Does it sound too good to be true? Do you want this? Come and get it! It is for you and free to get.

This is a command to love. It has just one simple rule, captured in one simple sentence: Love your neighbour as yourself. Yes, love your neighbour, you know, that man or that woman next door, exactly as you do love yourself. Are you very fond of yourself? Be equally fond of your neighbour. As simple as that.

Simple rule, isn't it? Or……..

The one I've seen probably being the best at this, is my dog Bibi. She is a wonderful dog, who's not only gorgeous, but also playful, very obedient, always happy. She is loyal and very kind to people, old and young. She is very intelligent and in no time she is able to convince almost everybody to love her. In all modesty, if not the best dog in the world, she is at least in the top 3.

Something that stands out about this kind of dog is their 'will to please'. No greater joy than pleasing their boss. This quality would make any employee the employee of the year. LOL!

So, should we all become like border collies? NO! Since at one essential part they totally miss the point. They please and please and will do so even to the point it'll kill them. They will keep going, keep running as long as their boss tells them. An inexperienced owner of a border collie can overlook how tired they actually are, to the point they could drop dead in their unstoppable will to please. I call this the "Border Collie Syndrome". And this is not how this command to love your neighbour as yourself is intended. We human beings need to love not only the other as ourselves. We also need to love ourselves as much as we love somebody else. Loving somebody else more than we love ourselves, is not sustainable. Of course, there are situations where we put the interest of somebody else above our own interest. Parents do a lot for their children. Or when we take care of a sick or dying loved one. For a while we can love more than we're being loved. And love isn't even asking for a scale so we can measure it to make sure it's equal. The essential word is not 'equal', it is 'balance'.

My take on this command is that we'll only be able to honour this as good as possible if we dare to be courageously self-compassionate. With our yes being as full of love as our no. To the other, to our self.

Journaling 'Border Collie Syndrome'

What does 'love your neighbour as yourself' mean to me?

What does 'love myself as my neighbour' mean to me?

Where do I suffer from the 'Border Collie Syndrome' and with becoming aware of that, what are the choices I want to make here?

51 Be happy. Be safe. Be well.

Towards the end of this book, where the intention from the beginning was to inspire you to make more conscious choices based on a further developed awareness, I want to dedicate a chapter with my longing for you.

Fair chance we don't know each other, nor that we will ever meet. That does not exclude my wish, my longing for you. Because you matter, whether we know each other or not.

What's a good friend? Of course there are many perspectives on this, yet things that come up for me, is that a good friend for instance, is a loyal companion who is willing to travel with you through life, whether you are the best version of yourself or not. A good friend will tell you when you screw up, like in your face, maybe be totally pissed off with you, yet love you nevertheless. Because a good friend loves you for who you are and is able to make the distinction between what you do and who you are. S/he will tell you that something you did is a total fuckup, yet that doesn't make you a total fuckup.

A true friend will tell you when you are playing small and encourages you to go for gold. Will champion you and hold you bigger than you dare to hold yourself. Just because you are you and they love you.

A friend will pick up the phone in the middle of the night when you call, knowing you need her, need him.

Your friends want you to be happy, to be safe, to be well. They want the very best for you and are compassionate to you. Maybe they don't like all your behaviours, yet they like you for who you are. Maybe they would love for you to become even more, or less, yet they are your friend for who you are right now.

In addition to the above, just take a moment what you see as the characteristics of what a good friend is. Write it down, before you

158

continue reading. Take your time for it. Seriously, stop reading and take your notes.

```



```

Done?

Now, we're going to change the game!

My longing for you is that YOU become your best friend. Yes, YOU!

Where you are compassionate to yourself. Where you are forgiving yourself after you screwed up, knowing that you are so much more than the mistake you just made.

Where you dare to take care of yourself, like you are the most important person in your life. Because no kidding, you are! Did you hear that? YOU are the most important person in your life!!

My longing for you is that you marinate self-compassion in self-authority. Where you dare to take a stand for yourself and speak from your authentic self. With power and authority. Because YOU MATTER! You matter so much that self-care is the logical consequence of self-compassion and self-authority. Of self-love. Because when you dare to love yourself, to take care of yourself, to be compassionate to yourself, to come from self-authority, you give the best possible version of yourself to your friends.

Journaling "Be happy. Be safe. Be well."

What is my definition of a friend?

How do I live up to this definition?

What is between you and becoming your own best friend?

52 I am complete

Somewhere in 2018 I got the vision to write this book. To capture my thoughts in words and share them with you. To inspire you. That was the intention. Maybe you could agree with my words, maybe you couldn't. As mentioned in the beginning, it never was about you agreeing or not! It was about triggering you to think about the issues touched upon in this book. To create a deeper awareness and that, from there, you would make up your own mind. Maybe the total opposite of what I wrote is your truth. Fine. It was about your authentic truth from scratch.

Writing this book was an experience in itself. After a long time of thinking about it, I just started capturing my thoughts. I confess I started writing with a deadline in mind, which I didn't meet. When I started writing on Serre de Poêt, somewhere in the vineyards near my house, I expected the process to go faster than it in reality did. That was one of the saboteurs I had to deal with.

Another one I had to fight was the one called The Perfectionist. That led to the choice to not ask an editor to correct my work nor a publisher to approve my words.

I apologize for all the miztakes, yet I trust that you got the message anyhow. And I hope it encourages you to start that project which you are procrastinating because of the perfectionist in you.

This book has been written at many different places, on several continents. At home, in the local café and in a cathedral. In at least three different continents. In my office and in nature. And like this final chapter, in airplanes. This made the process even more fun to me and also in line with who I am.

The word discipline, as mentioned in the beginning of this book, evolved into an even stronger commitment. I committed to myself and a few other people to transform this idea into a real book.

I had my moments where I didn't find the energy or inspiration to write. Then I allowed myself to pause, trusting life would inspire me through experiences to restart the writing and stick to the promise I made to myself. Not to anyone else. In that sense it was a selfish act...

This book is an expression of the purpose I see for myself in life: being an Awareness Builder who creates an army of positive change. When your life is positively changed in one way or the other through my words and your thinking about them, mission accomplished.

This book is an expression of self-care. I cared enough about myself to fulfil this longing.

This book is an expression of self-love. I loved myself enough to keep working on this so I could, one day, have that book in my hands and inhale the smell of that freshly printed paper and experience that feeling of accomplishment and pride.

This book is an expression of self-authority. To hell with all the obstacles, just do it! Not because I have to, yet because this is a longing for myself.

Thank you for reading this book.

Be happy. Be safe. Be well.
These are my words. I am complete.
Ho!

Journaling "I am complete"

What is expressing 'self-care' to me?

What is expressing 'self-love' to me?

What is expressing 'self-authority' to me?

Appendix 1: Sabogram

This is an easy tool to question the messages your Saboteurs are giving.
Follow the diagram and it's up to you who you allow to win. You or your
Saboteurs? Have fun with it!

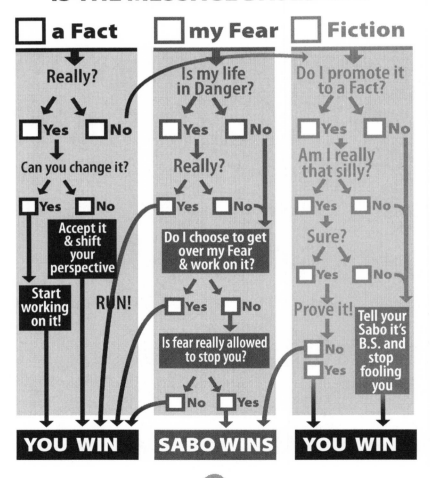

Appendix 2: Quotes

Here are some quotes from this book. Just for fun.

"A choice without action, is a just a useless thought"

"Discipline is a responsibility you can't delegate"

"The clock might stop, time never will"

"A phone becomes a smartphone when the owner knows when to turn it off"

"When you always want to be right, you will be left"

"Potential needs space"

39753726R00102

Made in the USA
San Bernardino, CA
21 June 2019